Comparison

Concepts in the Study of Religion

Critical Primers

Series Editor:
K. Merinda Simmons, University of Alabama

Books in the series Concepts in the Study of Religion: Critical Primers offer brief introductions to an array of concepts—modes of analysis, tools, as well as analytic terms themselves—within the discourse of religious studies. Useful for almost any course, the volumes in the series do not attempt to assert normative understandings but rather they introduce and survey the various modes and contexts for scholarly engagement with the concept at hand. How, for example, has the term "myth" been used, and what can various definitions allow us to do as scholars? Who in the field is working on the category of race and how? What might be the future of scholarship on gender in religious studies? What are the possibilities and limitations of description or comparison as methodological approaches? Thus, these critical primers provide—but are not limited to—concise overviews of the history of an approach or term. They also present the authors' own critical analyses of the dynamics and stakes present in discourses surrounding these concepts. Including lists of further readings to guide additional consideration of their topic, the books in this series are valuable resources for students and advanced scholars alike.

The series is published in association with the North American Society for the Study of Religion (NAASR).

Comparison

A Critical Primer

Aaron W. Hughes

SHEFFIELD UK   BRISTOL CT

Published by Equinox Publishing Ltd

UK: Office 415, The Workstation, 15 Paternoster Row, Sheffield, South Yorkshire S1 2BX

USA: ISD, 70 Enterprise Drive, Bristol, CT 06010

www.equinoxpub.com

First published 2017

© Aaron W. Hughes 2017

All rights reserved. No part of this publication may be reproduced or transmitted in any form or by any means, electronic or mechanical, including photocopying, recording or any information storage or retrieval system, without prior permission in writing from the publishers.

British Library Cataloguing-in-Publication Data

A catalogue record for this book is available from the British Library.

ISBN   978 1 78179 537 8   (hardback)
ISBN   978 1 78179 538 5   (paperback)

Library of Congress Cataloging-in-Publication Data

Names: Hughes, Aaron W., 1968- author.
Title: Comparison : a critical primer / Aaron W. Hughes.
Description: Bristol : Equinox Publishing Ltd, 2017. | Series: Concepts in the study of religion | Includes bibliographical references and index. | Identifiers: LCCN 2016055127 (print) | LCCN 2017036503 (ebook) | ISBN 9781781795392 (ePDF) | ISBN 9781781795378 (hb) | ISBN 9781781795385 (pb)
Subjects: LCSH: Religion--Methodology. | Comparison (Philosophy) | Religions--Comparative studies. | Religion--Study and teaching. | Judaism--Relations--Islam. | Islam--Relations--Judaism.
Classification: LCC BL41 (ebook) | LCC BL41 .H828 2017 (print) | DDC 200.71--dc23
LC record available at https://lccn.loc.gov/2016055127

Typeset by JS Typesetting Ltd, Porthcawl, Mid Glamorgan

Printed and bound in Great Britain by Lightning Source UK Ltd., Milton Keynes and in the USA by Lightning Source Inc., La Vergne, TN

Contents

	Acknowledgments	vi
	Preface	vii
	Introduction: A Personal Journey in and through Comparison	1
1.	To What Can I Compare Thee?	8
2.	History	25
3.	Possibilities	51
4.	Contexts	77
5.	Future	100
	Further Reading	115
	References	118
	Index	127

Acknowledgments

This slim volume had its origins in the 2016 Annual Meeting of the North American Association for the Study of Religion (NAASR) that was devoted to the topic of "Method Today." In addition to my paper on comparison, other papers were devoted to the topics of explanation (Ann Taves and Egil Asprem), description (Naomi Goldenberg) and interpretation (Kevin Schilbrack). I would like to thank the four respondents to my paper—Lucas Carmichael, Thomas Carrico, Drew Durdin, and Stacie Swain. I am also grateful to long-term conversation partners: William Arnal, Kalman Bland, Willi Braun, James A. Diamond, Jennifer Hall, Shaul Magid, Luther Martin, Russell McCutcheon, Steven Ramey, Matt Sheedy, Donald Wiebe, and Elliot R. Wolfson. Finally I would like to thank K. Merinda Simmons for including this in her series "Concepts in the Study of Religion," Hamish Ironside for copyediting the entire manuscript, in addition to Janet Joyce for her continued support of my work.

Preface

This little volume offers an introduction to one of the central methods that many maintain defines the academic study of religion: comparison. "To know one," F. Max Müller once famously quipped in the early part of the twentieth century, "is to know none." This phrase has functioned as the guiding inscription emblazoned upon the entranceway to the temple of religious studies ever since. Implicit in this locution is the idea that one cannot fully appreciate the breadth and depth of religion without putting at least two religions in counterpoint. It is their juxtaposition that is believed to show similarities, differences, and a host of other family resemblances. While this volume will put this assumption to the test, it is safe to assume that, by the end, comparison will be left standing. It will, I trust, be a somewhat different type of comparison than the kind that Müller had in mind over a century ago. If I could frame the volume in equally poetic terms, it would be along the lines of "she who knows one religion really well, knows that she cannot fall under phenomenology's spell."

Phenomenology—the study of various "things" (that is, phenomena), often cross-culturally, in order to appreciate the shared essence behind them—has governed much comparative work in religious studies since the term was initially coined by the Dutch scholar Pierre Daniël Chantepie de la Saussaye in 1887. The main problem with phenomenology, to be articulated more fully in the pages that follow, is its unwillingness to pay significant attention to specific linguistic and historical contexts. It is, instead, content to make a set of often superficial judgments about patterns of human religiosity based on insufficient attention to detail.

© Equinox Publishing Ltd. 2017

My slogan hints that, unlike Müller, comparison is a method that should be based on knowledge of one historical, textual, and geographic tradition. How, you may ask, can you compare one tradition to itself? Religions are such complex social forms that they differ based on temporal and geographical location. There is, for example, no universal Islam. What we find, instead, is a myriad of Islams that both overlap and differ from one another. So, rather than compare what Islam says about a certain topic (e.g., monotheism) with what Christianity says, it is often more productive to compare what various Islams say about a topic. If the phenomenological approach wants to lift ideas from contexts, my goal is to situate such ideas in localized and specific contexts.

The days of grandiose comparative schemas based on such superficial juxtapositions are hopefully coming to an end. In their place, I want to suggest, should be technically sound and theoretically rich contextual analyses that, though specific, both inform and are informed by other equally rich contextual analyses. In these localized contexts there is no need to talk of the divine, to make appeals to the sacred, or to use generic and formulaic expressions, such as "Muslims believe x." Rather, attention should be paid to how specific temporally and geographically located groups make meaning for themselves and how they do so, moreover, using a host of social, cultural, intellectual, economic, and other factors. Religious ideas, in sum, cannot be examined without sufficient attention to the various contexts that produce them.

Comparison is so implicated in all that we do that not infrequently we hear the name "comparative religion" as a synonym for religious studies. Indeed, my first job—at an institution that had one of the largest national chapters of "Campus Crusade for Christ," now apparently known as "Cru"—was in a department that went by that name. However, none of us really reflected on what it meant to be in a department of comparative religion, nor did we have a course or set of courses devoted to the task of comparison. Instead, faculty members used the term less as a designated methodology or as a coherent *raison d'être*, it now strikes me in hindsight, than as a signal, some sort of unwritten code, meant for administrators and Cru students that this was a serious academic department, and not one that engaged in religious studies' nemesis; to wit, theology.

This little anecdote illustrates, for me at least, the problem that this volume seeks to present and hopefully negotiate successfully. It is one thing to say that one does or engages in comparison, but it is something altogether different to reflect, both theoretically and systematically, on what comparison entails, what it can and cannot do, and what constitutes a good (or a bad) comparison. On the one hand, everything is comparable. I can, for example, compare myself to you, apples to oranges, night to day, the acting ability of John Goodman to that of Jeff Bridges, and so on. But, on the other hand, no two things are the same. I am *not* you, apples are *not* oranges, night is *not* day, and John Goodman's style of acting is *not* that of Jeff Bridges. Comparison, then, is the artificial act that brings two (or more) phenomena together *temporarily* and for the sake of some desired *end*. It is up to the comparativist to understand the what, the why, the when, and the how of putting two (or more) comparanda together. Too often this is not done, and we are told that (1) one religion, often one's own, is so unlike other religions that it is unique or *sui generis*. Or, at other times, we are told that (2) ultimately all religions are the same. Both of these, however, are ideological positions based more on polemics (the first case above) or apologetics (as in the second case).

The previous paragraph represents, in miniature, what my book will argue. All that follows seeks to unpack that paragraph by providing an extended analytical framework and by using a host of examples. In the process, I will encourage readers to reflect on the very act of what it means to compare by tracing the history and genealogy of the method, while simultaneously drawing on my own career working with Jewish and Islamic data in order to illustrate some of the finer theoretical points that I try to make. My argument is simple: comparison *can* be a useful method in the field of religious studies, but with the caveat that it has been greatly abused over the years. Comparison, as will become clearer in the pages that follow, can only occur under strictly controlled conditions and in specific contexts.

Following an introduction where I chart briefly my own adventures, both positive and negative, in comparison, my study is divided into five chapters.

Chapter 1 provides a basic introduction to comparison in religious studies. It asks, for example, what is comparison? Why do we compare, furthermore, and for what purposes? My goal in asking such questions is to set the stage for the remaining chapters that seek to work through this method's past, present, and future.

Chapter 2, "History," examines the use of comparison in the academic study of religion from a historical and genealogical perspective. It tries to show how too often comparison has been used superficially and to privilege certain religious expressions over others. Paradoxically, such endeavors are usually carried out under the guise of "science" or "objectivity." It offers several egregious examples, and seeks to show what is the matter with these examples' approaches and ends.

Chapter 3, "Possibilities," explores some of the possibilities and limitations of comparison as a methodology by looking at numerous contexts in which the method has been deployed. This will involve examining certain charged examples from comparison's past, such as Judaism and Christianity in the period after the destruction of the Second Temple period, and Judaism and Islam in the late antique period.

Chapter 4, "Contexts," argues that if comparison is to be a valid method in the contemporary academic study of religion, it must fulfill certain criteria: historical acumen and wide-ranging textual/linguistic dexterity. One cannot compare, to recalibrate Müller's phrase, what one does not know. The chapter pays particular attention to localized contexts by arguing that, unlike the approaches of yesteryear, comparison emerges from knowing one tradition very well and by reading outside of that tradition to see how scholars working with different data but with similar questions or problems deal with them. Comparison thus is the act of illumination, the ability to show that one's data is not *sui generis* but exemplary of a larger question of social meaning. Comparison, to return us to my slogan at the end of the first paragraph above, should not be phenomenological. It has to be grounded in the historical record.

The final chapter, "Future," looks into the crystal ball and tries to chart out a path for how comparison might well function in the academic study of religion in the coming years. While I argue, as I did in the previous chapter, that comparison must be a small-scale enterprise and based in history and textual sources, I also examine the two main holdouts to this approach. The first is, for lack of a better term, neo-phenomenology, which continues along the path of uncovering the sacred, albeit in ways that at least appear to be more sophisticated than previous iterations of the method. The second emerges from the domain of cognitive science of religion (CSR), which runs roughshod over the historical and textual record in its quest to ascertain pan-human cognition and behaviors.

* * *

Much of the thinking that went into this volume was developed out of a series of theoretical questions that emerged as I wrote *Shared Identities: Medieval and Modern Imaginings of Judeo-Islam* (Hughes 2017). That volume is a historical work that examines a number of sources produced by a set of overlapping and fluid social groups that emerged during the centuries following the death of Muhammad in 632 CE. While I have never considered myself to be a comparative religionist or someone otherwise engaged in the act of comparison, it became clear to me during the writing of that volume that I was both interested in and engaged with some of the questions that might roughly be classified as "comparative" in scope. So the present volume, which offers several extended examples lifted from that study, is an attempt to wrestle with some of the more theoretical issues raised there, but to which, for a number of reasons, I could not devote sufficient attention. Since I am a scholar of Islam and Judaism, I use these two religious forms, and the social groups that appeal to them, as my main data to think more theoretically about the task of comparison. Moreover, since my main argument is that comparison needs to emerge from an intimate textual and historical knowledge of specific traditions, readers will not find examples of me engaging in comparisons with traditions in which I cannot read sources in their original languages or in which I have but a fleeting knowledge of the historical record. To engage in such comparisons of which I have but superficial knowledge would undermine the central premise of this volume: to do comparison well one must not fall under phenomenology's spell.

Introduction

A Personal Journey in and through Comparison

I still remember my first encounter with comparison, at least as it intersected with the study of religion. It was 1988 and I was watching the PBS documentary entitled "Joseph Campbell and the Power of Myth," a set of six one-hour conversations between the late comparative religionist Joseph Campbell (1904–1987) and the journalist Bill Moyers. I was enthralled. In retrospect I am not sure why, but at the time the idea of a "monomyth," a universal mythic story, that linked the disparate cultures of the globe together combined with a cosmopolitan way of talking about places I had never visited impressed this intellectually starved teenager from the Canadian prairies. In the volume that came out of that series, *The Power of Myth* (1988), currently the number one bestseller on Amazon under the rubric "comparative religion," Campbell laments how knowledge has become increasingly specialized, so much so that scholars are either unwilling or unable to make connections between and across the disciplines that comprise the Humanities. He writes:

> Specialization tends to limit the field of problems that the specialist is concerned with. Now, the person who isn't a specialist, but a generalist like myself, sees something over there that he has learned from one specialist, something over there that he has learned from another specialist—and neither of them has considered the problem of why this occurs here and also there. So the generalist—and that's a derogatory term, by the way, for academics—gets into a range of other problems that are more generally human, you might say, than specifically cultural. (Campbell 1988: 11)

© Equinox Publishing Ltd. 2017

What undergraduate would not be interested in humanity over culture or worldly knowledge over specialized learning? For Campbell (and this is a leitmotif that winds its way through much of this literature) there are timeless and eternal themes—or, alternatively, Truths—that are given specific cultural "inflections" (*ibid.*: 13). While the specifics of mythic narratives may change over time and geography, he reasons that all represent but variations on one great story. This was an especially poignant discourse in the 1980s, the heyday of the *Star Wars* craze and its mythic invocation of the forces of good versus those of evil. Indeed, George Lucas, the creator of the series, was said to have been a "big fan" of Campbell, and the conversation between Campbell and Moyers even took place at his Skywalker Ranch just outside San Francisco. In his *Hero With a Thousand Faces*, Campbell is clear in his description of the role and the goal of the comparativist:

> to bring together a host of myths and folktales from every corner of the world, and to let the symbols speak for themselves. The parallels will be immediately apparent; and these will develop a vast and amazing constant statement of the basic truths by which man has lived throughout the millennia of his residence on the planet. (Campbell [1949]2008: xiii)

This idea of a universal truth, framed positively, looks for commonalities between religions of the globe, thereby providing some sort of pattern to diversity. Such a hermeneutic is idiosyncratic, to be sure: what is a pattern to one interpreter might be a coincidence to another. Comparison, now framed negatively, strips all cultural and historical specificity from myths and other social forms, and instead imagines all the world's great complexity as but a set of variations on a single theme. But, who gets to determine this theme? This is the great paradox of comparison. Do we seek unity in diversity or ought we to appreciate diversity for its own sake? It is also worth noting in this context that data do not "speak for themselves." On the contrary, it is interpreters who create their data based on an intricate and often hidden dialectic of privilege and denial. It is this dialectic more than anything that is ultimately responsible, if we retain the metaphor, for speaking to specific and often artificial situations.

Campbell was a strong believer in the psychic unity of humanity. Influenced by the late Swiss psychoanalyst Carl Gustav Jung

(1875–1961), he maintained that all people share on a fundamental level a basic level of consciousness, what is often called the unconscious or subconscious. It is this consciousness, he maintained, that functions as the "storehouse" of a set of panhuman ideas or archetypes. This panhuman storehouse, as we shall see later in this volume, is still alive and well in the academic study of religion, where it has recently been rehabilitated by the cognitive science of religion. At any rate, Campbell further argued that interconnected to this level of consciousness there exists an eternal source, whether this is the collective unconscious or something different, that helps us to make sense of time, of suffering, and ultimately of death. Myths—on Campbell's reading—provide the tear in the fabric of mundane reality whereby we are offered glimpses into the transcendent.

Stage two of my journey into comparison occurred in 1990, my second year of undergraduate studies. I enrolled in a "Theory and Method" course with the late Manabu Waida, who had been a student of Joseph Kitagawa (1915–1992) and Mircea Eliade (1907–1986) at the University of Chicago years earlier. It was a full-year course and we spent the entire second semester on Eliade's *Patterns in Comparative Religion* (1958). I was equally taken by this text, only being able to articulate my problems with the work much later. For Eliade, "the greatest experiences are not only alike in content, but often also alike in their expression" (*ibid.*: 3). This means that, for him, the scholar of religion is charged with tracing "not only the *history* of a given hierophany, but must first of all understand and explain the modality of the sacred that the hierophany discloses" (*ibid.*: 5; his italics).

A hierophany, literally "a manifestation of the sacred," represents for Eliade, as it would for his numerous students, a rupture into the quotidian, that which is signified as the profane. Imitating the language of Heidegger, who I was also fond of at this time, Eliade argued that the sacred, as something numinous and intangible, is what gives the world value, direction, and purpose by manifesting itself in various forms (e.g., stones, water, vegetation). The undefinable, and I would only appreciate this as a red herring later, is that which gives definition. Life, especially that of the primitive or rustic *homo religiousus* ("religious individual"), imitates and/or conforms to those hierophanies established "in illo tempore," namely the distant past (literally "at that time").

Eliade takes Campbell to the next academic level. The former was trained in an academic subfield (Hinduism) of religious studies and, at least in theory, knew some of the classical languages about which he spoke, whereas the latter seems to have been a dilettante going in many different directions at once, trying to find some common thread linking them. Yet, like Campbell, Eliade's cosmopolitanism and his seemingly endless knowledge of the world's religions—often equated with the great spiritual truths of humanity—again greatly impressed this young undergraduate especially at a time when I was on my own quest for knowledge and meaning. In retrospect, I have to ask myself, what did I find so appealing about the likes of Campbell and Eliade? Was it their universal cosmopolitanism? Was it the confidence with which they wrote? Was it their ability to draw a set of connections between disparate temporal and geographical phenomena? Was it the mysterious depths of existence to which their ideas pointed? Most likely it was some combination of all of these.

My intellectual context was soon to change, however. While I had glimpses here and there of the potential problems inherent to their approaches at the time, within a few years I became completely disillusioned. A critical, and dare I say more cynical, overlay would gradually replace my initial wonder. Where was the *history* in Campbell and Eliade, I began to ask myself? Is it possible to reduce human creativity and diversity to a "monomyth"? Did such a monomyth help me understand the often technical work I was doing in Islamic and Jewish philosophy, the subject matter of my subsequent doctoral work? What I had previously taken to be deep-thinking, I came to realize, was little more than a set of superficial pronouncements or, even worse, guesses.

My disillusionment also coincided with the beginnings of my own work in the languages (Arabic and Hebrew) that would go on to form the cornerstone of my own area of expertise. As I was learning how to read these languages, it dawned on me that neither Eliade nor Campbell could read a line of either language, yet they were quite content to utter a series of pronouncements about these two religions. If they did not take the time to learn the languages, then how could they really know anything about the textual, cultural, intellectual, and social diversity within these traditions? Where they were quite content to say something along the lines of "Judaism maintains x" or "in

Islam, this is tantamount to y," I always felt the need to nuance such gross generalizations. What Judaism or whose Islam were they talking about? No one working in the field of medieval kabbalah (Jewish mysticism), for example, would be so bold as to pronounce that "Judaism argues ..." If the likes of Campbell or Eliade did not know the history of these two religious traditions (including the diversity within each) *and* they could not read the languages associated with them, how could I be certain that they knew what they were talking about? This, I would soon learn, is the Achilles' heel of comparative religion, with comparativists not infrequently claiming knowledge about that which they probably have no business doing. Moreover, since they knew very little to nothing about the historical and textual traditions of specific religions, they could ostensibly make judgments to which no specialist in those religious traditions would assent. Maybe, *pace* Campbell, there is something to be said for the knowledge of the specialist after all.

It would only be several years later that I would begin to realize the political and ideological inflections of comparative religion. While there had been the occasional charges of anti-Semitism and right-wing leanings leveled against Campbell (see in particular Gill 1989 and Segal 1992), Mircea Eliade's close relationship to Romanian fascism in the interwar years became increasingly clear and documented after his death in 1986. According to Daniel Dubuisson, one of his foremost critics:

> [Eliade's] ontology is anti-Semitic because he wished to give an ontological basis (rather than simply a racist one) to anti-Semitism. He raises in opposition to these Jews—guilty of having created the modern world, materialism, science, and technology—the antithetical figure of homo religious, the European peasant who, still close to nature and its mysterious rhythms, intervenes ritually in order to maintain its "force" and "power." (Dubuisson [1993]2006: 219; see further Strenski 1987)

Mistrustful of the city and the pull of history, Eliade opts to romanticize the countryside, especially the cyclical time and eternal return of *Volkreligion* ("folk religion") found therein. The city is where the Jews were; and the countryside represented a pure and uncontaminated religious expression.[1] Yet if others criticized Eliade on ideological grounds, Jonathan Z. Smith has perhaps been his most forceful critic on an academic level. In his "Wobbling Pivot," for example, Smith (1978b: 88–103) notes how Eliade focuses too much on "sacred" centers and margins, and how he spends too much time on an "archaic/modern" dichotomy.

While this introduction is certainly not the place to get into problems with comparison in general and Eliade in particular, it is worth flagging in the present context that lurking behind the comparative enterprise is a fundamental essentialism that reduces groups, religions, and even races to generic or even stereotypical terms. This can lead to essentialisms that are not uncommon among certain nationalist thinkers and/or politicians. Just from the foregoing, we need to confront a basic question: Is it possible to salvage comparison from its previous investiture in a host of apologetic and ideological agendas? And, if so, how might we go about this? The chapters that follow seek to provide the background, context, and future of comparative frameworks in the academic study of religion.

I have recounted my "experiences" in this chapter because they are, I submit, exemplary to the journeys of many in religious studies. So many of us were drawn to the comparative frameworks of the likes provided by Campbell and Eliade. Their cosmopolitanism (European cosmopolitanism in the case of Eliade) and their ability to tap into the "timeless truths" of the world's religions struck so many of us as impressive intellectual feats and, for me at least, came at a transformative moment in my own intellectual journey. The key, though, is to see them for what they are, and what they represented to many of us with our own tortured relationship to organized religion. This means that the modern student of religion will, I hope, be more savvy than I was. The key to successful study, as I shall argue in the coming chapters, is specialized and technical study. While this may seem paradoxical (how, after all, can comparison be based on the particular?), it avoids the dilettantism and superficiality that plagues earlier comparative work. While attention to local contexts might make our collective endeavor more mundane, it is, I shall argue, but the first criterion for comparison.

Note

1. Lincoln (1999: 146), however, maintains that, as his student, he never once heard Eliade make any remark that could be construed as anti-Semitic.

Chapter 1

To What Can I Compare Thee?

To be human is to compare. Yet, comparison is both a natural and an artificial activity. It is natural in the sense that everyone compares. A successful striker in football, for example, is compared both to other strikers and to his or her own form the previous year. Parents compare the growth of a child, to use another example, to that child's siblings or friends. The value of a painting is decided in comparison to other paintings whether by the same artist or others. So, whether we like it or not, or even whether we admit it or not, we are constantly engaged in some form of comparative activity. To know is to compare. It is, of course, also to assign value.

At the same time, and this is one of the great paradoxes, to compare is also to engage in an artificial activity. Lionel Messi is not Pele; I am not my brother; Vincent van Gogh is not Andy Warhol. To put the latter term in each of these dyads in counterpoint with the former means that we have to strip away each individual's particularities in order to focus on one specific issue; for example, goals scored, height/weight, and monetary value. Never mind that Messi currently plays for Barcelona in La Liga (the Spanish premier division) and Pele played with Santos in Brazil over 50 years earlier; that I am a university professor who lives in Rochester, NY and my brother a landscaper in Edmonton, AB; or that van Gogh is a French impressionist and Warhol an American pop artist.

In each one of these instances, it is important to be clear just what is to be gained by the comparison. Do we engage in comparison to say that one is better than another? But better at what? In the case of Messi and Pele, is the comparison based on natural footballing ability

© Equinox Publishing Ltd. 2017

or on number of goals scored? The comparison would look rather different in each instance. Who had better supporting players? Who faced weaker opposition? How are footballs or football boots today different than those from over half a century ago? If we are not clear on why we engage in a certain comparison, we may well be unconsciously skewing the results or stacking the deck to prove that which we presumably already know to be the case. A comparison, then, is never self-evident even though those who put it forth into the world are convinced that it is. It is, on the contrary, something fleeting and impermanent, something that is meant to fulfill some temporary purpose. Messi's skill level, for example, may compare with that of Pele in certain instances, but not others. Other than that, of course, they are completely different individuals, playing in different positions, in different countries and in different leagues, with and against different teams, and complete with their own set of worries and concerns off the pitch.

To what, then, can we compare comparison? It is, if nothing else, a literary conceit: an activity that selects, juxtaposes, and manipulates two or more unrelated objects that an individual perceives to share one or more similar or overlapping characteristics. On a poetic register, these characteristics can be as obvious as comparing love to a rose or as arcane, as in the hands of Donne, of comparing love to the two legs of a drafting compass.[1] The goal of such comparisons is presumably to invoke a sense of wonder in the reader by showing the interconnectedness of the natural world and by enabling her to see one thing in terms of another.

Yet, to show the resemblance of two different objects, it is necessary to explicate the logic that comprises the comparison and try to illumine why and how they are held together. Love is neither a rose nor is it a drafting compass. Yet, if one wants to talk about love, describe it, and analyze it, one presumably needs metaphors and a comparative grid on which to plot it. It is for this reason, to reiterate, that comparison is a natural way to describe the world in which we live. If we described everything simply on its own terms—if we even could, *pace* the philosophical phenomenology of Edmund Husserl or the youthful Martin Heidegger—we would live monochromatically and we would certainly be the worse off for it. But, at the same time, our ability to hold two or more things together in our mind creates a host of epistemological and ontological problems that we must ultimately confront. Since literary conceits portray one thing as something else, they make sense on the level of the imagination, but the intellect demands clarification. Although such clarificatory skill is not necessarily in the job description of the poet, it is (or at least ought to be) in that of the academic.

While there are certainly good comparisons and bad comparisons, common to both is the sheer artificiality of the enterprise. This stems from the notion that if two things are exactly alike, then they must necessarily be the same thing (see Neusner 1991: 175). Since no two things can be exactly alike—love is not nor ever can be a drafting compass; Messi is not Pele; Islam is not Judaism—it is up to the juxtaposer or the comparativist to tell us *why* they resemble one another. And, just as importantly, (1) *when* they do, (2) for *how* long and (3) for *what* purpose. Too often, however, these latter aspects are muted and, in the academic study of religion at least, this frequently results in a model in which specific religions are imagined to manifest timeless and disembodied truths. One religion (and it is usually a religion and never a particular subset of one) is either like or unlike another religion. Traditional comparison, then, has been involved in distilling an essentialized concept—*the* Jewish concept of prayer, for example—and then showing how it is either similar to or different from the same concept in another religion, staying with the above example, *the* Hindu notion of prayer. Comparison, in other words, essentializes and reifies objects and actions, often without due attention to contexts, with the aim of neatly comparing and contrasting them to one another.

The academic study of religion, to be sure, is certainly a more mundane and quotidian affair than poetry. There are, objections of some to the contrary, neither Donnes nor Celans who can make us imagine the world anew by drawing a set of comparisons between disparate social expressions signified as "religious" by their practitioners. Instead, as we shall witness in the pages that follow, comparison in our chosen field has been used for a host of apologetic and often highly ideological ends. So much so that many now doubt its utility (e.g., Smith 1982; Patton and Ray 2000: 1–4). Too many times we have read articles or monographs that purport to tell us how *x* in one religion resembles, is similar to, or is different from *y* in another. What, if anything, we have to ask ourselves, is gained by such an activity? Despite all the bad and faulty comparisons that litter our field, is it worth proceeding? If yes, we need to think about what a responsible comparison might look like. In many ways, the answer has to be yes because, in lieu of or despite our best intentions, there is something comparative built into the way we know and describe things. Things can and do remind us of other things, and since we engage our world comparatively, comparison remains a natural part of our cognition. However, and this is the paradox, *while the comparative act might be natural, specific comparisons are not.*

Comparison: The Good, the Bad, and the Ugly

Unfortunately, comparison habitually finds itself gravitating towards two ends of an ideological continuum: either (1) to show how two or more things are either entirely different or (2) to demonstrate how they are essentially the same. Despite their rather different ends, however, the hermeneutic that informs them both would seem to be based on a set of often extra-scholarly concerns.[2] If the former not infrequently wants to show how one's own religion is superior to others (e.g., the Christ-event is qualitatively of a different nature to those of, say, mystery cults of antiquity), the latter is informed by a set of irenic concerns premised on interfaith or interreligious dialogue (e.g., "Abrahamic religions should be able to get along because they all emerge from Abraham").[3] But we all know, or at least should know, the results of such endeavors. The field is cluttered with such intentionally faulty and self-serving comparative studies. A quick search on Google Scholar, for example, returns reams of titles using comparison in this manner, some of which will be surveyed below, from the late nineteenth century to yesterday, from the premodern to the postmodern, and from the ridiculous to the sublime. With few exceptions, these works all revolve around the assumption that comparison is or can be a valid method in the field. However, very rarely do such studies actually take the time to reflect on the theoretical concerns and baggage that are ultimately part and parcel of the comparative act.

But to compare comparative schemes and to choose which one offers the best model is perhaps not the best way to proceed. I will suggest a few historical antecedents in the following section, but allow me now to begin with my argument: *If comparison is to be an effective method it must be historical and not phenomenological, local and not global.* By this, I mean that while cross-cultural comparisons may appear eye-catching or useful ("*x* in Hinduism," for example, "is like *y* in Christianity"), such results are at best idiosyncratic, that is, contingent on the particular needs of the comparativist, and rarely if ever verifiable. A much more useful type of comparison is one that emerges from those places where contiguous or overlapping social groups speak the same literal language and think with the same metaphorical vocabulary. Since these localized interactions not infrequently occur on the margins, they tend to give definition to centers. Since they are marginal, however, they are often overlooked or written off as non-normative. This is why comparison must be both a self-reflexive and a self-critical enterprise: why, for example, compare this, but not that? Or, why compare something from the third century CE with something from the fourteenth? Such questions must both be answered and theorized.

History provides one of the greatest antidotes to the type of essentialist reifications that have plagued and continue to plague religious studies and that result in the most egregiously superficial frameworks of comparison.[4] The historical record bequeaths to us actual and verifiable material, textual, economic, political, intellectual, and social interactions between groups. Lest I appear as a historical positivist and claim that "the facts do not lie," it should go without saying that historians are often not the most theoretically sophisticated when it comes to comparative frameworks. Instead, I wish to suggest that *comparison ought to be located at the intersection of historical data and theoretical sophistication.* To do history like a historian (complete with linguistic and cultural expertise) and engage in social theory like a social theorist is, for me, the perhaps unattainable goal of comparison in religious studies.

It is at this point, however, that we run up against the outer limits of our chosen discipline. The greatest task for those of us who work in religious studies is to translate between the highly technical specifics of our chosen subfield (e.g., South Asian studies or medieval Islamic philosophy) and the often too general framework provided by our disciplinary home.[5] If the former is detail driven and cautious, the latter often encourages us to speak and write about specific religions (e.g., "Islam," "Judaism"), and to transform them into categories of analysis. A quick perusal of course offerings in any given department should bear this out. We see courses like "Introduction to Islam" or even "Introduction to Sufism (Islamic Mysticism)," but rarely courses devoted to specific geographical areas or temporal periods. At what point, we might well ask ourselves, is a study too technical, of interest to only a few other specialists, or when does it become too general and unrecognizable to fellow specialists outside of religious studies? The latter, it will be recalled, was the problem endemic to the work of Joseph Campbell and Mircea Eliade. Balancing these two opposing sides of the continuum is never easy. Those engaged in comparison must write for two perhaps mutually exclusive audiences: those who work in the specific era and texts that are being compared but who are not scholars of religion and those interested in questions supplied by religious studies but not necessarily in the same historical timeframe or geographical context.

As someone who works on the interface of, for lack of better terms, "Judaism" and "Islam," presumably I work on comparison. Though I have never called myself a "comparativist" or someone who engages in the task of "comparative religion," I guess I am and I do. I imagine I have not defined myself as a comparativist because, by and large, I do not see myself as doing the type of essentialist comparative work that usually goes by this name in religious studies. In what follows I want to use some of my own work that deals with the interaction of various social groups who define themselves in some way as "Jewish" or "Muslim," with the aim of teasing out a second-order set of reflections. My work on these two traditions is not to "compare" a generic or heuristically constructed Judaism with an equally generic or heuristically constructed Islam to ascertain some sort of theological or interfaith ends based on essentialist categories (e.g., prophecy or messianism). Instead, I find it much more productive to look at the interactions of specific groups at specific times and in specific places—often underdefined groups that speak the same language, create similar social worlds in response to the same political uncertainty, and seek to define themselves in light of the other. Before I do this, it might be worthwhile to examine some egregious examples endemic to the comparative enterprise.

Comparison as Protection

At the very beginning of his *Introduction to the Study of Comparative Religion*, Frank Byron Jevons (1858–1936)—the Principal of Bishop Hatfield's Hall at the University of Durham—could write as follows:

> The use of any science lies in its application to practical purposes. For Christianity, the use of the science of religion consists in applying it to show that Christianity is the highest manifestation of the religious spirit. To make this use of the science of religion, we must fully and frankly accept the facts it furnishes … It is by faith in Christianity that the missionary undertakes to convert men to Christianity. The comparative value of different religions can only be ascertained by comparison of those religions. (Jevons 1908: ix–x)

Here we see a number of problems, many of which are not confined to the first decade of the twentieth century but that continue into the present. The first is that the study of religion is conflated with the term science, making it sound more objective than it actually is. While the term "science" in German (i.e., *Wissenschaft*) can be and frequently is applied to the various fields and disciplines that comprise the Humanities (e.g., *Wissenschaft des Judentums*, or Jewish studies; *Religionswissenschaft* or the study of religion), Jevons is writing in English. The implication, of course, is that he is signaling to his readership that there is something inherently objective or value neutral about what he is about to do. Whatever he is about to undertake, he informs his reader, is objectively true and independently verifiable. It soon becomes quite clear, however, that nothing could be further from the truth. The pinnacle of Jevons's analysis and the underlying reason for his comparison is to demonstrate that which he already holds to be self-evident, namely, that Protestant Christianity is the epitome of religious expression known to humankind. The study of comparative religion, on his reading, does not create a temporary framework to illumine a particular facet of comparison; rather, it creates cold, hard facts that are meant to be objective, universal, and scientifically verifiable to the "disinterested" observer.

In order to prove the superiority of Protestant Christianity, not surprisingly his own religion, Jevons must put all religions on an evolutionary scale, from the most rudimentary to the most perfect. This evolutionary approach to religion, as J. Z. Smith reminds us, is one of the major ways of arranging data in the field of religious studies (see Smith 1978a: 259–264). For Smith, while this provided the guise of science, it was, in fact, anything but. He writes:

> A careful examination of the works of the cultural evolutionists will reveal no principles of organization or comparison. The meticulous arrangement of series, the micromovements and variations so essential to the biological evolutionists' work, were totally lacking in the studies of their cultural counterparts. (Smith 1978a: 260)

To return to Jevons: Though "there is nothing to compel us to assume that the lowest form in which religion is found was necessarily the earliest to exist," he continues, "it is convenient for us to start from the lowest forms" (Jevons 1908: x). This desire to put religions on such a scale is one of the hallmarks of the academic study of religion,[6] a feature that has stained the enterprise for much of its history. If religions can be put on a grid from the least to the most sophisticated, so, too, can those who practice them. The history of the academic study of religion has, perhaps not surprisingly, been caught up in the project of racism and colonialism (see, e.g., Chidester 1996, 2014), in addition to anti-Semitism (see, e.g., Hughes 2013). This means that the white and the Christian (always signified as Protestant Christianity) becomes the lodestar against which other "Western" (especially Judaism), "Eastern," and indigenous forms are put in counterpoint (see Masuzawa 2005). The latter, not surprisingly, are always found wanting.

In a set of lectures presented on behalf of the American Lectures on the History of Religions (ALHR), and later published as *Religion of Israel to the Exile* (1899), Karl Budde compares early Christianity to the Judaism that came before it.[7] Whereas the latter was "at first crude, [it] grew constantly in purity and elevation till at last, in the progress of revelation, [it] reached the lofty spirituality of the New Testament" (Budde 1899: 1). However, there are, according to him, kernels of this lofty, universal aspect found earlier than the New Testament in prophetic books such as Deutero-Isaiah and Micah. Despite the existence of this universalism in such books, he subsequently argues, this religion "was not at that time fulfilled, and [their] extravagant promises retired into the background for a long time under the pressure of the post-exilic conditions of Jewish life" (*ibid.*: 216). Such a message, one endorsed by the ALHR no less, is perhaps not surprising given Budde's own religious and professional proclivities. His comparative scholarship, again, conflates with what he knows to be true, namely, that the Old Testament would—indeed could—only find its fulfillment in the coming of Jesus Christ and his messianic prophecy that would build naturally upon the universalism of Isaiah, particularly Deutero-Isaiah. This universalism, in Budde's eyes, was able to transcend naturally the particularism found in more "ritualistic" or "legal" books (presumably those like Leviticus and Deuteronomy). He writes in the grand conclusion to his lecture series,

> Can we conceive of any sharper contrasts than we find between the world-wide, glowing universalism of Deutero-Isaiah and the narrow, icy particularism of Ezekiel—between the ritualism of Ezekiel and the complete superiority of Jeremiah and Deutero-Isaiah to all external cult—between the resignation of Jeremiah and the enthusiastic expectations of the other two—between the inner life of God in Jeremiah and the worldwide sublimity of the God of Ezekiel? ... It has pleased God to give His human children the noblest and most beautiful flower of His revelation, the Gospel of His Son Jesus Christ. (Budde 1899: 217–218)

For Budde, studying the religion of ancient Israel is not an end in and of itself. It is only worthwhile when compared to Christianity, which is assumed to perfect it. The religion of the ancient Israelites shows the ancient roots of Jesus' message and, in the process, the ultimate uniqueness of that message. Judaism had it but did not realize it, whereas Christianity did.

Returning to Jevons, we read that for "the practical purposes of the missionary it is desirable where possible to discover any points of resemblance or traits of connection between the lower form with which his hearers are familiar and the higher form to which he proposes to lead them" (Jevons 1908: x). The goal of comparison, simply put, is to show the superiority of Christianity, and to reveal to non-Christians why they are "backwards" and how they might change this unfortunate state of affairs. Again, we see how missionary work, subjectivity, and discussions about civility and barbarity are all folded under the "scientific" cover provided by a seemingly objective account of comparing disparate religious forms.

A survey of the world's diverse religious expressions, according to Jevons, informs us that if

> we recognize that the end of religion, viz., communion with God, is an end at which we ought to aim, then the process whereby the end tends to be attained is no longer evolution in the scientific sense ... As a fact, the missionary everywhere sees arrested development, imperfect communion with God ... The Christian theory of society again differs from all other theories in that it not only regards the individual's composing it as continuing to exist after death, but teaches that the society of which the individual is truly a member, though it manifests itself in this world, is realized in the next. (Jevons 1908: xxv)

A question we could ask is, why does Jevons believe that communion with God is the "end" of religion? His own religion does, of course. A Jew, a Buddhist, and a Hindu might object. But such an objection would be that of an "inferior" religious form so it could easily be written off—as Budde did with Judaism after the emergence of Jesus—as unable or unwilling to realize the true nature of religious expression. Again, we see a scholar of religion under the guise of putative objectivity elevate what he considers to be the telos of religion and then use it as the principle to compare and contrast different religions. Development is only "arrested" because it does not conform to his own understanding or that of Christianity's. Here we see clearly how the idiosyncratic whims of the comparativist dictate the analysis. Perhaps this is another way of saying that it would appear that Jevons knows his conclusions—that his form of Christianity is superior to all other religions—before he even begins his analysis. All of this, of course, takes place under the guise of science and objectivity, and anyone who disagrees with him either misreads or misinterprets the evidence that he marshals.

But what is left out of such a comparative approach? We are never informed. We hear a lot about science, a lot about the work of the missionary, a lot about the developmental superiority of Protestant Christianity. Who gets to decide? Since Jevons does not know the languages of those religions to which he compares his own, how can he (and thus we) be certain that the translations accurately represent the original. Why, in addition, does he choose one text from Judaism, but not another. We, the readers, are never presented with such a rationale despite the assurances that scientific method is guiding his analysis. Instead, we must take Jevons at his word. Jevons originally delivered the lectures that would become his *Introduction to the Study of Comparative Religion* at the Hartford Seminary in Connecticut. This seminary, he informs us, may be "the first institution in the world which has deliberately and consciously set to work to create by the courses of lectures, of which this series is the very humble beginning, an applied science of religion" (Jevons 1908: 1). His audience, like the author himself, are Christians who share the proclivity for the superiority of their own tradition.

Although it has become trendy again to speak of the study of religion as a "science"—for example in the cognitive science of religion—we must ask ourselves what is scientific about Jevons's work. He endeavors to tell us when he differentiates between "pure" science (that which discovers facts) and "applied" science (that which uses them), and informs us, unashamedly and unabashedly, that his business is "to use the discovered facts as a means of showing that Christianity is the highest manifestation of the religious spirit" (*ibid.*: 2). There is, however, not a shred of anything we might label as "scientific" about such a method.

Comparison and the Isolation of the "Sacred"

If the likes of Jevons and Budde sought to protect their version of Christianity by creating the terms by which it could and could not be compared, the more recent trend in the academy has been not so much to protect a particular religion, but to investigate and try to locate the more inclusive sounding "sacred." This approach was being developed almost as early as Jevons's "scientific" use of comparison. In 1917, less that ten years after Jevons published his *Introduction*, Rudolph Otto (1869–1937), professor of theology at the University of Marburg, published his path-breaking *Idea of the Holy*, one of the most influential books on comparative religion published in the twentieth century.

Otto defines the "idea of the holy" as the "numinous," a term he uses to refer to an "unnamed Something," that which lives as "the real innermost core" of all religions, and "without it no religion would be worthy of the name" (Otto [1917]1923: 6). This non-rational feeling that he believes to be present in the world's religions is what inspires awe in practitioners. The numinous, thus, functions as the basic framework for the comparative enterprise. Since all religions represent but external forms or manifestations of the numinous, they must, at root, be similar to one another. Catholic, Protestant, Muslim, Jewish, Buddhist, Hindu, and even local indigenous traditions thus represent distinct embodiments or manifestations of this non-rational category, which for Otto can be reified into an object of analysis (*ibid.*: 143–154).

On one level, this would seem to be a major development from the comparative approach that we witnessed in the likes of Budde and Jevons. Otto, for example, never talks about the work of the missionary, nor does he invoke the term "science" as a panacea. If anything, Otto encourages us to move beyond rationality as embodied by such concepts and instead insists that we should devote our time to examining the pre- or non-rational.

This does not mean, however, that there are not problems associated with Otto's use of comparison. First, Otto's method, like his contemporaries, is impossible to qualify or quantify. How can one base a comparison on that which is an inner feeling? Can the scholar verify that one has had a numinous feeling? This "feeling" or "experience," to this day, remains at the heart of comparison. As we shall witness in the final chapter, neo-phenomenologists still invoke comparison to get at some undefined and amorphous sense of the "sacred." Because it is undefinable, it can be defined in the images of those doing the investigating. Moreover, all particularities, and this is a leitmotif we shall see throughout this study, are stripped away so that an essential and experiential core can be located. History is ignored, particular contexts are overlooked—yet both of these features are responsible for the generation of so-called "religious" texts. Whereas the study of religion should be interested in how such mundane forces generate such texts, phenomenologists and neo-phenomenologists are more interested in seeing such texts as "divine" and repositories of the world's collective wisdom. Finally, as problematic as Jevons and Budde, we witness Otto's belief that the purest expression of this numinous is, unsurprisingly, located in Protestant Christianity. In the conclusion to *The Idea of the Holy*, for example, we read,

> Every religion which, so far from being a mere faith in traditional authority, springs from personal assurance and inward convincement (i.e., from an inward first-hand cognition of its truth)—*as Christianity does to a unique degree*—must presuppose principles in the mind enabling it to be independently recognized as true. (Otto [1917]1923: 175; my italics)

Without getting into the technicalities of this utterance, I want only to focus on the word "unique." This one word, as we have seen throughout this chapter, has unfortunately clouded much comparative work. If something is unique in the taxonomic sense then it belongs to no taxon and is, for all intents and purposes, unknowable. But this is not what Otto means. Instead, "unique" for him becomes a category of analysis that simultaneously enables him to show the superiority of Christianity, his own religion, or to remove it altogether from the comparison when it suits him—not unlike what Jevons was doing. Since Christianity possesses ideas and concepts to a "unique degree," we have to understand that it drives Otto's analysis. He looks at his own religion, decides what is best about it, and then uses this as the term of reference to look at the other religions of the globe. Although the latter are found to possess the numinous, they can in no way manifest it to the degree that Christianity can.

Others would pick up on Otto's numinous where it would subsequently be referred to as the "sacred." Paramount in this regard is perhaps one of the most influential thinkers of religious studies over the course of the twentieth century, someone we already encountered in the Introduction, Mircea Eliade. For Eliade, the sacred is the polar opposite of the profane and, as for Otto, is equally difficult or impossible to define. "But as soon as you start to fix limits to the notion of the sacred," he writes, "you come upon difficulties" (Eliade 1958: 1). Since the sacred is that which cannot be explained or analyzed in its pure state it must be studied in its various manifestations. It is the latter that point to the former, again conceived of as the pure essence of religion. Although this essence is defined by its absence and what it is not, mundane phenomena point toward it. This, however, is the reason for engaging in the comparative enterprise: diverse phenomena provide various articulations of the sacred in order to unlock it and show the latter in all of its presumably unknowable complexity. In his introduction to *Patterns in Comparative Religion*, Eliade writes:

> It is just such a comparative study that we want, for only thus can we discover both the changing morphology of the sacred, and its historical development. In embarking, therefore, on this study, we must choose a few among the many religions which have been discovered by history, or ethnology, and then only some sort of their aspects or phases. (Eliade 1958: 1)

Again, though, we run up against problems. Social or religious forms are important only insofar as they point beyond themselves, to the so-called "sacred." This means that historical, political, ideological, and economic features, to name only a few, are largely ignored because they either take away from or are completely irrelevant to the sacred. But, again, who gets to decide what is important and what is not? The interpreter, of course, who is, once again and perhaps not surprisingly, the one who works under the guise of scientific objectivity. The profane nature of the modern world is largely uninteresting to Eliade, except insofar as it functions as the foil to and potential site of manifestation of the sacred. Each appearance of the sacred, a "hierophany," thus reveals some modality of the sacred (but the hierophany in no ways exhausts it), at the same time that the hierophany's appearance in history "reveals some attitude man has towards the sacred" (*ibid.*: 2).

While Eliade would at least seem to acknowledge the concept of history—given the fact that he was instrumental in creating the *history* of religions at the University of Chicago's Divinity School—it is again largely absent or, at the very least, subservient to the sacred. Eliade, then, is not so much interested in why things happen or in demonstrating historical causality as he is in understanding the sacred, that which ultimately transcends history. He thus uses history selectively or, in his own words from the previous block quotation, "only some ... of [its] aspects or phases." The question becomes, what aspect or phases? Why some but not others?

This rather idiosyncratic methodology means that every "religious" phenomenon points to or is reducible to some sort of hierophany. Because of this, all forms relating to a particular morphology (e.g., vegetation, the waters, time, space) can be compared with one another. In speaking of the sky and sky gods, for example, he writes:

> Fortunately, religious life, and all the creations that spring from it, are dominated by what one may call "the tendency towards an archetype." However many and varied are the components that go to make up any religious creations (any divine form, rite, myth or cult) their expression tends constantly to revert to an archetype. We shall be able, for that reason, to glance at some of the sky gods of polytheistic religion *without having to know the "history" of each in order to understand his make-up and his career*; for each one, whatever the history that has gone before, tends to work back to his original "form," to revert to his archetype. (Eliade 1958: 59; my italics)

Here, Eliade shows just how unimportant history and the historical record is to his comparative enterprise. The presumed archetypal structure behind the world's various and manifold sky gods, for example, means that the historical construction of each specific deity is largely unimportant. Social, cultural, economic, political, and other forms can all be marginalized, I would suggest, because they get in the way of the story that Eliade wants to tell. This story is the familiar phenomenological one that desires to describe the manifold ways in which the "sacred" appears to human beings across religious traditions, and the various ways in which humans understand, to return us to Otto's term, the numinous.

In the pages that follow I wish to suggest that the comparative enterprises of those like Jevons and Eliade are problematic in the extreme, albeit for different reasons—Jevons for his largely apologetic framework and Eliade for his phenomenological one. Indeed, if comparison is to remain viable in the academic study of religion and not simply as a means to non-intellectual ends, then it is incumbent upon us to reflect on the activity and then set out the theoretical parameters in which it can be carried out successfully.

Conclusions

This introductory chapter has revealed something of the task and paradoxes of comparison: its naturalness, its artificiality, its failure, and its potentialities. Neither Jevons and Budde on the one hand, nor Otto and Eliade on the other, are outliers, but official representatives of the two major approaches to the comparative project—the apologetical and the phenomenological—that continue to be used with considerable regularity to this day. Both approaches, to reiterate, were (and still are) haphazard and sloppy, and the basis for comparison in each is never articulated except in the fuzziest of ways.

If we are to move beyond such approaches, however, we need to remember several things. The first is that history cannot simply be invoked or ignored when it suits the comparativist. History, on the contrary, is what prevents the type of gross essentializations witnessed already in this chapter. One cannot talk about "Judaism" (or "Islam" or any other religion), for example, in a way that implies a generic "Jewish" mindset, namely, that there is a Jewish way of thinking. If anything the historical record presents us with a myriad of often contradictory Judaisms. The second is that one should be upfront about why one is comparing in the first place. If one wants to engage in a theological project of showing the superiority of one's own religion, why not just confess that this is one's aim and avoid all the comparisons and pseudo-comparisons with other religions. Third, comparison tends to be done for ulterior motives and presented under the guise of scientific objectivity. Finally, and relatedly, there is always some element that the comparativist hides from view. This hermeneutical sleight-of-hand privileges and denies data. The question then becomes: how is it possible to move beyond such, at first blush, terminal problems that would seem to undermine the entire project of the comparison of religion?

The remaining chapters will try to address such issues head-on.

Notes

1. See John Donne, "A Valediction: Forbidding Mourning":

   > If they be two, they are two so
   >   As stiff twin compasses are two;
   > Thy soul, the fixed foot, makes no show
   >   To move, but doth, if the other do.
   >
   > And though it in the center sit,
   >   Yet, when the other far doth roam,
   > It leans, and hearkens after it,
   >   And grows erect, as that comes home.

2. Jonathan Z. Smith has done more than anyone to bring attention to these extra-scholarly and extra-curricular agendas. His concern, however, is primarily with the first of the two uses I have described. For him, this involves the uniqueness (e.g., the "Christ-event") of what one is trying to compare:

   > Here the "unique" is more phoenix-like, it expresses that which is *sui generis*, *singularis*, and, therefore, *incomparably* valuable. "Unique" becomes an ontological rather than a taxonomic category; an assertion of radical difference so absolute that it becomes "Wholly Other," and the act of comparison is perceived as both an impossibility and an impiety. (Smith 1990: 38)

3. For my critique of the category "Abrahamic Religions," see Hughes (2012).
4. On the problematic use of history in the "history of religions," see McCalla (1994) and Lincoln (1991).
5. This is where problems emerge. Even those who do not work on comparison *per se* nevertheless work in a discipline—if, in fact, religious studies is a discipline—predicated on a comparative framework that has been used and abused for a host of non-scholarly agendas.
6. Jonathan Z. Smith labels the "evolutionary" as one of the four main approaches to the study of religion, with the others being the ethnographic, the encyclopedic, and the morphological. Of the evolutionary, he writes:

   > Comparative religion as it was practiced in the nineteenth and early twentieth centuries was essentially an illegitimate combination of the older morphological approach to comparison and the newer evolutionary frame of reference. As among the older comparative morphologists, the comparative religionists held that structures were to be studied and compared without regard to chronology and geography (or speciation, for that matter); but rather as to an increased order of complexity. (Smith 1978a: 260)

7. This paragraph reworks Hughes (2013: 88–90).

Chapter 2

History

This chapter seeks to present some of the historical uses to which comparison has been put over the centuries. Temporally, it spans from the fifth century BCE to roughly the present—from antiquity to postmodernity via the late antique and medieval periods—and its cast of characters includes Herodotus, Justin Martyr, al-Shahrastani, and Émile Durkheim. Following the lead of the late J. Samuel Preus, I wish to argue that the authors treated here represent a "coherent research tradition" (Preus 1987: ix) that has, with a few exceptions, employed comparison for distinct ends, namely, the manufacture of some sort of normativity or orthodoxy, be it religious or intellectual. What follows provides a concise and perhaps idiosyncratic overview of the history of comparison. What has been at stake? How has the category, if not the actual term, been deployed over the centuries? And, perhaps most importantly, for what purposes has comparison been invoked over the years?

There have been many attempts to locate the origins of the comparative study of religion. Daniel Boyarin (2014), for example, has tried to argue that comparison began as a heresiographical enterprise as Christian theologians attempted to eradicate the fuzzy borders, both semantic and social, between Judaism and Christianity in the late antique period. He argues that comparison was invoked by the political desire to ascertain heresy (e.g., Judaism and Judaizing Christians) and the concomitant need to establish Christian orthodoxy. Those groups of Christians who believed what was in the process of becoming normative doctrines and engaged in similarly constructed normative practices could be labeled as orthodox and all those Christians (e.g., Gnostics, Monophysites, Arians) and Jewish Christians that did not became signified as heretical. Comparison thus functioned as a way to categorize groups by ascertaining which groups conformed to what was slowly coalescing as orthodoxy and those that did not. It is important to note in this context that this was a political as opposed to an intellectual let alone a religious process. The main objective of comparison was to firm up the lines between what had previously been considered overlapping social groups: Jews and Christians on the one hand, and normative and heretical forms of Christianity on the other.

Another attempt to locate the origins of comparative religion is offered by Steven M. Wasserstrom (1988, 1995), who argues that comparison between distinct religious groups occurred not in the late antique period, but in the medieval Islamic one. Central in this regard was, once again, the tradition of mapping heretical groups (i.e., the genre of heresiography), only this time those associated with medieval Muslim thinkers. Most important in this regard was al-Shahrastani (1066–1153), sometimes dubbed the "first historian of religions." Since Islam was a religion of the law, the legal standing of various social groups needed to be worked out. What better way to do this than to classify such groups according to their religious beliefs? Like their late antique precursors, medieval Muslim heresiographers were in the business of establishing orthodoxy by ascertaining how various internal and external groups compared with the normative one (i.e., Sunni Islam). Again it is worth noting that, for al-Shahrastani, comparison was a legal activity that determined who did or did not have to pay the poll tax (*jizya*) levied upon non-Muslims.

Still other scholars want to put the origin of comparative religion much later and locate it instead in early modern Europe. Guy G. Stroumsa (2010), for example, maintains that the rise of European empires, and the encounter with foreign lands and customs, led to an interest in ethnological study. When coupled with the Reformation and the invention of philology, he argues that we witness the creation of our modern concept of religion and, just as importantly, the establishment of a "new science" (i.e., comparative religion) that sought to categorize and understand the many religions of the world.

Still others want to put the origins of comparison in the context of the modern world, where it went hand-in-hand with quantifying, qualifying, and categorizing religions other than one's own. David Chidester (1996, 2014), for example, connects this desire to the colonial period, especially on the frontiers of empires, such as South Africa. In such places, different customs and religions, often constructed as "primitive" when compared to Europe, had to be understood for the sake of colonial manipulation and governance. This investiture in colonialism and empire maintenance, in turn, created the trope of "primitives" and "primitive religions" that would go on to play such a large role in theories of religion being created in metropoles such as Vienna, Paris, and London.

Russell McCutcheon (1997) locates another chapter in the history of comparison in the *sui generis* discourses associated with phenomenologists such as the already encountered Rudolph Otto and Mircea Eliade. Such individuals sought to demonstrate how a spiritual and ahistorical essence—alternatively named as the holy or the sacred—manifested itself in diverse religious traditions and practices. Yet others, like Bruce Lincoln (1999), Horst Junginger (2008), and Stefan Arvidsson (2006), have demonstrated the connections between the academic study of religion, comparison, and the rise of fascism in the interwar years as modern nation states attempted to define and manufacture those traits that defined a people over and against others.

Comparison (and this takes us back to a theme that should hopefully now be familiar) has rarely been about disinterested scholarship. If anything, comparison has been embroiled, depending upon the time and the place, in a host of political, ideological, legal, colonial, and nationalist debates. In the process, comparison has been used to privilege and deny certain forms over others, thereby elevating and marginalizing certain expressions. Not infrequently those forms and expressions singled out for comparison are purely idiosyncratic, and the result is a set of gross essentializations that seeks to reduce complexity to simplicity. There is no way to finesse the fact that the academic study of religion in general and its method of comparison in particular has been used for a host of apologetic and nefarious agendas.

The present chapter seeks to explore in greater detail some of these historical moments by illumining their immediate contexts, operational assumptions, and main players. Common to all of these diverse moments is that in order to compare, there has to be something normative against which the comparison takes place. Witness Jevons's assumption that Protestant Christianity was normative and all of the religions of the globe paled in comparison to it. This normativity, in other words, is always associated with those who initiate the comparison—they are, after all, the ones who desire the comparison in the first place, they control the comparanda (i.e., that which is to be compared) and the terms of reference, and they are the ones who privilege and deny. Historically, this initiation emerges from a dominant group, such as Protestant Christianity or Sunni Islam. Comparison, one could say, is the conceit of the powerful.

To invoke a thought experiment, however, there is no reason to assume that if a Trobriand Islander should find herself transported to the Vatican, she would want to compare her tribal religion to what she saw in Rome and, of course, would assume her own tradition to be the normative one. Comparison then takes place in such a way that one's own traditions maintain their superiority—why else would they be one's own tradition?—at the expense of other religions with which they are put into counterpoint. Except for our imaginary Trobriand Islander, the result is pretty much always and everywhere the same: comparison becomes a prerogative of the dominant and protects the interests of the dominant.

Comparison and the Creation of Self

Comparison with others is one of the major ways that social groups define themselves. We do x, for example, whereas others do y or z. Since we, whosoever we might be, do x, it must be natural, and y and z must be seen as somehow abnormal or strange, and ultimately interpreted in its light: Why is it different? What does it resemble? And so on. In this respect, comparison is an attempt to account for the different, the incongruous, and the exotic. "Something other has been encountered," in the words of Jonathan Z. Smith (1978a: 246), "and it is surprising either in its similarity or dissimilarity to what is familiar 'back home'." Comparison, framed somewhat differently, begins with the acknowledgment of difference and the simultaneous attempt to overcome it. However, and not infrequently, the individual engaged in the comparison understands his or her own tradition to be the normative one or somehow representative of the correct way of doing things.

In his *Histories*, for example, the fifth-century BCE Greek historian Herodotus could write:

> Persians hold fire to be a god. To consume corpses with fire then is by no means according to the custom of either people, of the Persians for the reason which has been mentioned, since they say that it is not right to give the dead body of a man to a god; while the Egyptians have the belief established that fire is a living wild beast, and that it devours everything which it catches, and when it is satiated with the food it dies itself together with that which it devours: but it is by no means their custom to give the corpse of a man to wild beasts, for which reason they embalm it, that it may not be eaten by worms as it lies in the tomb. (Herodotus 1890: book III, §16)

Here, Herodotus describes for his Greek readership how the different people with whom he has presumably had direct encounter, envision fire from a religious perspective. Persians imagine it one way, and Egyptians another way—both in a manner that presumably differs from how Athenians imagine it. Comparison, for Herodotus, is based on a first-hand encounter with others and represents an attempt to overcome the cognitive dissonance that emerges therefrom. Comparison is non-scientific, to be sure, and is frequently based on a set of anecdotal musings used to explain, often after the fact, random encounters. To use the words of Smith again, "such comparisons are idiosyncratic, depending upon intuition, a chance association, or the knowledge one happens to have at the moment of another culture" (1978a: 248–249). For example, consider the following description from Herodotus:

> The Egyptians were the first who made it a point of religion not to lie with women in temples, nor to enter into temples after going away from women without first bathing: for almost all other men except the Egyptians and the Hellenes lie with women in temples and enter into a temple after going away from women without bathing, since they hold that there is no difference in this respect between men and beasts: for they say that they see beasts and the various kinds of birds coupling together both in the temples and in the sacred enclosures of the gods; if then this were not pleasing to the god, the beasts would not do so. (Herodotus 1890: book II, §64)

Note how Herodotus describes what the Egyptians do and then compares it to a similar practice that the Greeks (i.e., Hellenes) do. He subsequently compares it negatively to the temple practices of other social groups that he has observed. But, and this is key, we have no way to verify independently the information. We must take him at his word. There is, then, nothing systematic about the comparative act. There is nothing we can independently verify. In ancient Greece, not unlike today, we have to take the comparativist's word for it. We must assume that he or she has accurately relayed the information—information that is not infrequently based on chance encounters and spontaneous interactions no less—to us.

This example from Herodotus introduces several features into the history of the use of comparison. The first is that it shows us that comparative religion is by no means a modern phenomenon. In many ways, it cannot be since it is bound up with alterity and the encounter with those that can be described as "not like us." It thus functions as a crucial ingredient in the definition of self. Another example of this use of comparison comes by way of all those biblical verses that seek to show the difference between the cultic practices of the ancient Israelites and those of their polytheistic and idolatrous neighbors. This represents yet another very earlier iteration of comparative religion. But, and this is the second point, both the Bible and Herodotus work on the assumption that their own practices are the right ones and those that do not share them are either *barbaroi* (i.e., barbarians) in the case of the Greeks or pagans in the case of the ancient Israelites. There is, in other words, always a value judgment implicit in comparison. Third, both of these examples show us how comparison is used to classify others using oneself, one's social group, one's religion, and one's values functioning as the lodestar.

Comparison as Heresiology

One of the earliest forms of comparative religion, if we can use that term anachronistically, is, as we have just witnessed, located in the genre of heresiology, namely, the categorizing of heresies. I say "anachronistically" since those engaged in the documentation of heresies certainly did not perceive themselves to be engaged in the activity that we today call comparative religion. Rather, they imagined themselves as engaged in the practical work of defining orthodoxy (i.e., themselves) by studying and documenting the teachings of various sects (i.e., others) that had the potential to threaten the status quo and that could subsequently be written off as "heterodox." Again, we see the importance of categorization at the heart of the comparative enterprise. In their quest to establish an imagined normativity, heresiologists and other theologians created, established, and patrolled orthodoxy, deciding who or what fitted and who or what could be proscribed as "heterodox" or even "heretical."

While that which heresiologists practiced and believed was, not surprisingly, considered to be normative, the practices and beliefs of those with whom they disagreed for a host of political and ideological reasons became constructed as non-normative. Heresiologists and other theologians were, then, ultimately responsible for the definition of which groups could be located safely within the community of believers and which ones could not. Prior to such activities on the part of heresiologists, however, heterodox groups were not surprisingly imagined as part of the community of believers (see Brakke 2011: 5–8).

Yet if heresiology gives one of our earliest examples of comparative religions, it might also offer us a second-level order of instruction into the uses of taxonomy. Instead of using a model in which stable religions interact with one another, indeed as the heresiologists themselves imagine the interaction, it might be more profitable to think of various social groups who inhabit a common cultural space wherein beliefs are not infrequently broadly distributed. Ultimate distinctions between religions—including who is inside and who is outside—are created by what Daniel Boyarin (2014) refers to as later "border markers"—heresiologists, theologians, among others—eager to construct discrete identities for their fellow practitioners. In so doing these "border markers" moved individuals, groups, ideas, and behaviors to one side or another of what was then, but not later, an artificial border (*ibid*.: 13–17). In his own words,

> Therefore with respect to religious history we must add yet another factor ... to wit, the activities of certain writers/speakers who wish to

> transform the fuzzy category into one with absolute clear borders and the family resemblances into a checklist of features that will determine an intentional definition for who is in and who is out of the group as it defines itself and, therefore, its others. (Boyarin 2014: 26)

Boyarin's own work, as we shall witness in greater detail in Chapter 4 below, is interested in how second and third century heresiologists engaged in a process of creating difference between Judaism and Christianity. But we also see a similar logic at play in early Islam, where heresiologists also sought to taxonomize the beliefs of others, again for reasons that we might describe as distinctly nonacademic. Indeed, Eric J. Sharpe's *Comparative Religion: A History* credits one of these individuals, al-Shahrastani (d. 1153), as responsible for "writing the first history of religion in world literature" (Sharpe 1975: 11) in his *Book of Religions and Sects* (*Kitāb al-milal wa'l-nihal*). In the introduction to the work, al-Shahrastani informs us:

> Our treatment shall cover Islamic sects and others who have a truly revealed book, as the Jews and Christians; those with a book of somewhat similar kind, as the Magians and Manicheans; those who have penal laws and statutes but no book, as the ancient Sabaeans; and, finally, those who have neither book nor penal laws nor religious laws, such as the earlier philosophers, atheists, star-worshippers, idol-worshippers, and Brahmins. (Quoted in Wasserstrom 1988: 407)

The section of the work that addresses non-Muslim religions begins with revealed religions, about which al-Shahrastani discusses four groups of Jews and three groups of Christians. He then moves out to survey religions that consider themselves to be revealed but who acknowledge that they only possess scriptures that they themselves (and not Islamic theologians) consider sacred.

It is worth noting, however, that this use of comparison—perhaps like comparison in general—is never value neutral or done for its own sake. Indeed, as Wasserstrom has pointed out, Muslim heresiography of the Jews (and, of course, others) was employed for legal and political purposes (Wasserstrom 1988: 410). This could include the creation of oaths for legal purposes, in addition to tax collection. Comparative religion thus was necessary for the grouping of minorities within their appropriate category of the civil law. It was necessary, according to Wasserstrom, for "legists needed to know who was a Muslim, a member of a tolerated community, or an 'other,' inasmuch as different laws applied to each of these categories" (*ibid.*).

Comparative religion, for al-Shahrastani, was not determined simply by disinterested scholarship, although intellectual interest and curiosity may well have played a role in his endeavor, but ultimately based on the legal subjugation of others. This is something that we shall witness time and again in this chapter: comparison is invoked not to show similarity, but to reveal disparity between one's own religion (witness Jevons in the previous chapter) and those of others. One's own religion, not surprisingly, is imagined as normative and subsequently constructed as such. Those of others are imagined as the opposite. That opposition must be subsequently documented and categorized. Comparison now becomes the method used to show difference and to accentuate their otherness, all the while paradoxically using that distinction and otherness for self-definition.

One would like to think that this was unique to the premodern world, something that preoccupied heresiologists in their futile attempts to create orthodoxy and stamp out or at least circumscribe all that threatened it. Such, however, is not the case. Comparative religion has been embroiled, as Chidester (1996, 2014) whom I mentioned earlier, reminds us, in empire maintenance and the categorization of groups (like-us and not like-us) in order to control them. This time, however, the borderlines are not ideological but geographic, and the "border guards" are not heresiologists but colonial administrators, many of whom were scholars. Knowledge of others, as Foucault reminds us by way of Edward Said, is tantamount to power over them (Said 1975: 3). This is not necessarily a matter of cause and effect—"as if the study of religion could cause imperial expansion," in the words of Chidester (2014: 312)—but a situation in which knowledge of other religions was based on issues of normativity, authenticity, and ultimately about maintaining imperial stability.

In this, it is perhaps worth noting that comparative religion is always enacted and performed by the dominant. Unlike their Muslim counterparts who classified them in great detail, for example, Jews did not classify or categorize the various Islams that they encountered. This is not unlike the way Protestant Christianity positions itself in the contemporary field of religious studies by providing a set of guidelines by which other religions measure themselves or are measured by others (see Fitzgerald 2000: 3–32).

A Modern Conceit

If much of the premodern interest in the comparison of religions was bound up with establishing orthodoxy by virtue of defining its despisers, the modern world has had a somewhat different set of interests in the activity. This does not mean though, as witnessed previously, that modern thinkers do not distinguish between low (i.e., indigenous religions), higher (e.g., Buddhism, Judaism) and the highest (i.e., Protestant Christianity) forms of religion. Despite the guise of greater disinterest and an engagement with the activity for the sake of a putative scholarly sense of objectivity, it nevertheless often remains, as we shall see, a distinctly partisan endeavor. Comparison, not surprisingly, continues to reflect the religious prejudices and cultural conceits of those who undertake the activity.

Within this context, Protestantism has largely become the religion to which other religions are compared and ultimately made to conform (see Dubuisson 2003). Predicated on faith, good works, and individual salvation, Protestantism is held up as the universal and that to which other religions should aspire if not ultimately become. When they are held up to a set of spiritual virtues that are not their own, these religions are, needless to say, found wanting. If Protestants, for example, engage in silent and orderly prayer in church, traditional Judaism with its "shockling" (swaying back and forth), loud, and apparent unorderly prayers appears aesthetically unappealing and, by extension, inferior. Or, when an exact analogue cannot be found in another religion, something that is believed to be similar in the mind of the comparativist is posited. The result is that the religions of the globe are all imagined to be pale imitations of Protestant Christianity and ranked as such on an evolutionary scale with the latter on the top (see Masuzawa 2005).

F. Max Müller (1823–1900) is generally regarded as the founder of the modern study of comparative religion. Perhaps best known for the phrase with which I began this book, "to know one is to know none," Müller was interested in, among other things, examining the origins of Aryan (also known as Indo-European) languages and comparing them based on their similarities. It might be worth noting that Müller wrote at a time when scholars were beginning to posit a direct relationship between language, linguistic groups, and cultural development. The early twentieth-century discovery of the Indo-European language group led to much speculation about the relationship between numerous ancient peoples and the relationship between Europe and the ancient Vedic culture of India. Comparative work between European and Asian languages led many to believe that Sanskrit represented the earliest of the documentable Aryan languages. Existing somewhere behind Sanskrit, it was believed, there existed a proto-Aryan language, which was the source of all the others, still often given the name *I-E (i.e., "proto-Indo-European").

It was within this larger context that Müller devoted himself to the study of Sanskrit, translating many of its texts (including the Rig Veda) into English for the first time, thereby establishing himself as one of the major Sanskrit scholars of his day. As was common among his contemporaries, Müller connected language to religion, and the subsequent development of language to the evolution of religion. Vedic religion, he argued, was a form of nature worship and that the gods of the Rig Veda represented active forces of nature that had been personified as deities. This led to his famous claim that mythology was "a disease of language," which transformed natural concepts into supernatural beings and stories.

Allow me to illustrate with an example. Various Aryan gods, Müller argued, began as expressions of abstract ideas that were subsequently personified as deities. The Aryan father-god, to be more specific, appears under various names: Zeus (in Greek), Jupiter (in Latin; derived from *deus-pater*), and Dyaus Pita (in Sanskrit), all of which can be traced to the proto-Aryan *Dyaus* meaning "shining" or "radiant." We thus see an evolution from the general concept of radiance to generic sky deities like Deus or Theos, to wit, "the radiant one," and then to distinct and now recognizable gods such as Zeus and Jupiter.

Müller's relation to India, however, was somewhat complicated. He never travelled there and apparently forbade his students from doing the same because, for him, the "real" India existed only in ancient texts (Sugirtharajah 2003: 47–48). If anything, he seems to have seen his own work in Indian texts as a way to unlock an originally pristine and ancient wisdom that had been fettered by more modern and cultural practices (see Bryant 2001: 285–290). In a letter to his wife, for example, he writes:

> The translation of the Veda will hereafter tell to a great extent on the fate of India, and on the growth of millions of souls in that country. It is the root of their religion, and to show them what the root is, is, I feel sure, the only way of uprooting all that has sprung from it during the last 3,000 years. (Müller and Müller 1902: 328)

Virtually every comparative religionist—from Müller to Eliade and beyond—has tried to locate a primordial and presumed universal aspect of religion in the ancients. They subsequently argue, as we shall see shortly, that the way to understand these ancient religious experiences is to examine their modern analogues among "primitives" (e.g., Australian aboriginals, North American first nations, Trobriand Islanders), or among rural dwellers (in, e.g., the Romanian countryside). Comparison has frequently become invested in the project of modern European nationalism by showing how the present, when compared to the greatness of the past, is found wanting.

Comparison and Nationalism

The academic study of religions, as we have just seen, is obsessed with origins. The intersection of modern metropolitan life and the need to find ostensibly "premodern" cultures to offset it or make it more spiritually meaningful has had a tremendous if often unacknowledged impact on the rise and popularity of the academic study of religion.[1] Nationalism and regeneration have often coincided in this field of study and this intersection has frequently meant the need to find earlier iterations of present desires in more "primitive" forms that can then paradoxically be located and plotted on an imagined historical record (see, for example, the essays in Junginger 2008). This could mean "locating" an Aryan Jesus in history (see Heschel 2008: 26–66), or it can mean, as is so common today in certain circles, discovering primitive democracy in ancient Israel (see, e.g., the critique of this in Hughes 2015b).

Within this context, another towering figure in comparative religion in the twentieth century was the Italian Raffaele Pettazzoni (1883–1959). Through his many important scholarly works (for bibliographies, see Gandini 1960 and Casadio 2011), he sought to reorient the field from its ahistorical and phenomenological origins to, what he hoped, would be something more historical (see Ciurtin 2008; Prandi 2012). He was one of the first historians of religions in Italy, where he held a chair at the University of Rome. Internationally, Pettazzoni served as the second President of the International Association for the Study of Religion (later renamed as the International Association for the History of Religions or IAHR), and he was one of the founders of the academic journal *Numen* and its corresponding book series Studies in the History of Religions, both still published by Brill. Pettazzoni, in other words, did much to create the scholarly infrastructure of the history of religions both in Italy and beyond.

Pettazzoni's most famous monograph is *The All-Knowing God: Researches into Early Religion and Culture*, the translation of his 1955 *L'Onniscienza di Dio*. This work broke with received scholarly opinion that maintained that monotheism was the *Urreligion*, as posited by the likes of Andrew Lang (1844–1912) and Wilhelm Schmidt (1868–1954), from which polytheism "degenerated." While Pettazzoni found evidence of monotheism in primitive societies, including the recognition of a supreme being, he argued that there was no evidence that such beings were recognized to the exclusion of other spiritual entities. He thus challenged the notion that these supreme beings were monotheistic gods. One finds, he argued, supreme beings defined in many ways, such as the bringer of rain, the protector of the hunt, or even as the mother earth in agrarian societies. Distinct historical situations, he argues, create distinct supreme beings.

Pettazzoni claimed that the basic thesis of "primitive monotheism" conflated theology and history, and he instead argued that monotheism is but a recent religious development and that just because many polytheistic gods were all knowing, this need not equate with monotheism, primitive or otherwise. Despite his pioneering historical researches into the topic, however, Pettazzoni's method is today generally seen to be of the phenomenological variety, essentially ignoring the historical record in favor of making superficial comparisons between unrelated datasets (see, e.g., Nanini 2003, 2012; Prandi 2012).

It is also important to remember, given the tenor of this section, that Pettazzoni was a colleague of Giovanni Gentile, the self-described "scholar of fascism," at the University of Rome (see Severino 2002). According to some of his papers, Pettazzoni refers to Gentile as his benefactor at that institution, and as the person who was able to secure the funds for his professorship. In 1925 the "Istituto Giovanni Treccani" was established in Rome. Named after the wealthy industrialist who sponsored its activities, one of the institute's main goals was to publish a national encyclopedia that was modeled on the *Britannica* and other nationalist encyclopedias (see Turi 2002). The goal of the project was to bring all of Italy's cultural and intellectual expressions within the embrace of fascism. The director of the entire project was Gentile, and he appointed Pettazzoni to organize History of Religions and Folklore for what would eventually emerge as the *Enciclopedia Italiana di Scienze, Lettere ed Art* (see Stausberg 2008a, 2008b).

In 1938, Pettazzoni signed the so-called *Manifesto della razza* (or "Charter of Race"). Within fifteen years of the establishment of fascism in Italy, as Pettazzoni himself notes in the *Civiltà fascista*, the official mouthpiece of the Institute of National Fascist Culture, the history of religions was officially established at six universities and taught at ten (Pettazzoni 1938: 194). The fascist regime even encouraged Pettazzoni to hold the 1940 Congress of the International Association for the History of Religions (IAHR) in Rome. Though it never happened on account of the war, the regime offered him $50,000 to organize it. It seems that the regime used Pettazzoni's international fame and his research into "primitive" religion—especially "primitive" Italian religious forms—as a way to legitimize itself. It also seems that Pettazzoni did not mind this so long as his scholarship was not compromised. It is around this time that we see Pettazzoni begin to work on religion in rural Italy (e.g., Pettazzoni 1912), and, especially, in the late 1930s and 1940s, on the city of Rome, which he argued "was the central point of reference for the entire history of religions" (Stausberg

2008a: 382). For Stausberg, Pettazzoni's language echoes that found in Mussolini's understanding of Rome, which played such a large role in fascist mythology, and also Gentile's concept of *Romanitá*.

Pettazzoni's connections to Italian fascism are echoed in many other European historians of religions of this period. These include, as we have seen, Eliade's relationship to Romanian fascism. Another towering figure of mid-twentieth century comparison was Georges Dumézil (1898-1986), someone with ties to French fascism. Dumézil, a comparative philologist, was perhaps best known for his "trifunctional hypothesis," which posited the existence of three classes or castes—priests, warriors, and farmers—that correspond to the three functions of society: the sacred, the bellicose or martial, and the economic (see, e.g., Littleton 1973: 7-20). Bruce Lincoln and others, however, have accused Dumézil of supporting a hierarchical order that was inflected by contemporaneous French fascism (Lincoln 1991: 231-243; 1999: 121-137). Lincoln further argues that modern French nationalists on the "new right" have subsequently picked up Dumézil's fondness for order and repudiation of egalitarianism. According to him,

> Those on the New Right ... cite Dumézil's writings in support of their positions—their fondness for hierarchy and authority, for example, their antipathy toward egalitarianism and the ideals of the Enlightenment, or their triumphal view of "Indo-Europeans" as superior to all other peoples—we may suspect them of appropriating nothing other than positions of the Old Right that have been brilliantly recoded and misrepresented first as ancient wisdom, and second as scholarly discourse. (Lincoln 1999: 137)

Comparison has thus long been invested in a host of nationalist causes. In this regard, as we have witnessed in this section, comparison is a method that allows an interpreter to locate an idyll in a distant past and subsequently show how it can aid in the regeneration and rehabilitation of the present. Connections between the present and an imagined distant past show how a people has a unique calling and that this past makes a group distinct from others. The essentialization of such utterances has played a large role in the history of the comparative enterprise.

Comparison as Evolution

Müller, Pettazzoni, Eliade, Campbell, and scores of others have been interested in the comparative enterprise to uncover what they consider to be some originary experience or universal consciousness. Since such an originary experience can never be uncovered in ancient religious forms, for no other reason than that we lack direct access to them, many comparativists have looked to modern "primitive" religions. These contemporary primitive religions, often code for indigenous traditions in places such as Australia or North America, are then used to provide insights into the earliest stages of religious development. They are assumed, in other words, to show us what are believed to have been our earlier stages of cognitive and social development. Since they have yet to be theologized or philosophized, the so-called primitive religions are believed to offer simpler expressions of religious life. In their simplicity, in other words, we see what the "high" religions might have looked like at the moment of their origins.

Edward Burnett Tylor (1832–1917), the English comparativist, argued in his *Primitive Culture* (1871) that it is "survivals" that hold the key to unlocking the past. He defines survivals as those aspects of culture that "have been carried on by force of habit into a new state of society different from that in which they had their original home, and they thus remain as proofs and examples of an older condition of culture out of which a newer has been evolved" (*ibid.*: 15). Survivals thus function as modern conduits that lead directly into ancient practices. In his own words:

> The thesis which I venture to sustain within limits, is simply this, that the savage state of mind in some measure represents an early condition of mankind, out of which the higher culture has gradually been developed or evolved, by processes still in regular operation as of old, the result showing that, on the whole, progress has far prevailed over relapse. (Tylor 1871: 28)

We also witness this correlation between contemporary primitives and our direct descendants in the ancient world in the work of Émile Durkheim (1858–1917) who studied the religion of Australian

Aboriginals (albeit from the comfort of his own armchair) in order to provide a set of analyses on religion writ large. In the opening paragraph of his *Elementary Forms of the Religious Life*, he writes:

> In this book we propose to study the most primitive and simple religion which is actually known, to make an analysis of it, and to attempt an explanation of it. A religious system may be said to be the most primitive which we can observe when it fulfills the two following conditions: in the first place, when it is found in a society whose organization is surpassed by no others in simplicity; and secondly, when it is possible to explain it without making use of any element borrowed from a previous religion. (Durkheim [1915]1965: 13)

This is not a simple historical exercise, he informs us, because his goal—as someone engaged in the "positive science" of sociology—is to know and reconstruct earlier forms of civilization. It may seem strange that "one must turn back, and be transported to the very beginnings of history," he writes, "in order to arrive at an understanding of humanity as it is at present" (*ibid.*: 14). Durkheim himself compares this to the discovery of unicellular biology, which has "transformed the current idea of life since in these simple beings, life is reduced to its essential traits, they are less easily misunderstood" (*ibid.*: 19).

Obviously there is an evolutionary model here that interlocks with a comparative one. Religions are assumed to evolve, to develop structurally, and to be complicated on account of subsequent theologizing. Comparing later forms—presumably the "world" religions—to contemporary "primitive" forms enables us to see what the former would have looked like at an earlier stage of their development. In studying them, we study ourselves.

But note the paternalism in such a model. It is always assumed that "primitives" have simple religious forms. It is further assumed that they have something called "religion" (i.e., some sort of spiritual and inner experience devoid of social, cultural and other contexts). Here we need to remember that "religion" is a modern term, one with its own distinct genealogy in the political history of the West, and one moreover that has no real equivalent in other cultures (for an important critique of this assumption, see Dubuisson 2003: 9-16). It is us who have elevated a category that is a product of the West and forced other cultures to isolate those aspects that we have deemed to be "religion" or "religious." "How was a typically Christian notion," Dubuisson asks, "initially used in a very particular, anti-pagan polemical context, able to become a scientific concept suitable for use in the framework of a vast, crucial anthropological reflection" (ibid.: 24)? He continues:

> The West not only conceived of the idea of religion, it has constrained other cultures to speak of their own religions by inventing them for them. Religion is not only the central concept of Western civilization, it is the West itself in the process of thinking the world dominated by it, by its categories of thought. (Dubuisson 2003: 93)

A central feature in this construction and dissemination is comparative religion. As we have seen one of the defining features of comparison—whether in Herodotus, the heresiologists of the late antique period or medieval Islam, or modern historians of religion—is to signify that which is normative and that which is not. Greek cultic practice, Orthodox Christianity, catholic Sunnism, Protestantism, and cosmopolitan Europe all—at one time or another, in one way or another—have fit the bill.

Ecumenicism: The Other Face of Comparison

If much of this chapter has focused on the various ways that comparative religion has traditionally sought to assign value, and thus as a way to uphold truths that are perceived to be self-evident, we must not lose sight of the fact that, especially in recent years, comparison has been used ecumenically to show that all religions—and thus all peoples—are ultimately the same. This model plays off of the Eliadean paradigm that we have already encountered, but has certainly been given a renewed emphasis in light of world events ushered in by the attacks of September 11, 2001, and all that has followed in their wake. This model, to reiterate, envisages an eternal and timeless sense of the "sacred" of which all religions and religious forms represent but manifestations. If Eliade conceived of comparison, the primary method to articulate the morphology of the sacred, to be an academic activity, many who engage in this activity in the modern period often do so under the guise of theology or inter-faith dialogue. Though they often imagine themselves as engaged in scholarly (now used as a buzzword in the same manner that Jevons used "science") comparison, the intentions and results of their endeavors are often anything but.

Comparison in the name of some inter-faith ecumenism is predicated on a negative theology that seeks to name something that cannot be named and give definition to that which by virtue of its putative transcendence cannot be defined. Different religions, despite the fact that they may appear to be significantly unalike, are in the hands of such ecumenical comparativists shown to be essentially similar. One such egregious example comes by way of the 2007 *Unity in Diversity: Interfaith Dialogue in the Middle East* published by the United States Institute of Peace. The authors—Mohammed Abu Nimer, Amal Khoury, and Emily Welty—write the following:

> Jews, Muslims, and Christians share and identify as fellow pilgrims on a path—a path all three faiths understand to be profoundly rooted in concepts of truth and peace. Adherents of the Abrahamic faiths believe that right conduct is essential and that sacred texts hold instructions about how to live an ethical, just life that is pleasing to God. Jews, Christians, and Muslims share the belief that God wants them to live a life full of respect for justice, peace, and human relationships. All three believe in the validity of revelations as a sign from God and struggle to maintain unity in spite of splits in their populations (Reform/Orthodox, Shiite/Sunni, Protestant/Catholic). (Abu Nimer, Khoury, and Welty 2007: 19)

This passage, as I hope should be clear even without my commentary, is full of gross essentializations of each of the three religions, which then receive an even grosser essentialization when they are all imagined as "Abrahamic." It is as if there is some "Abrahamic" ethos that, if rediscovered, should be able to get these three religions to sit down together in the name of a peaceful and shared patrimony. Again, this Ur-Abrahamic religion is as illusive and as nebulous as the Urreligion posited by the likes of Müller and Tylor. In the passage just cited, individuals from the three traditions are described as "fellow pilgrims" who share a similar notion of revelation, which in turn leads to a common quest for truth and justice. Diversity within each tradition is papered over, as are the differences between them. This is because—and here it is necessary to reiterate one of the features that has traditionally plagued the use of comparison in the study of religion—history takes a backseat whenever the comparativist wants to make a non-historical point. The historical record is either ignored completely or used selectively. Notice how even the sectarian movements within each tradition—Reform/Orthodox, Shiite/Sunni, Protestant/Catholic—are assumed to be qualitatively the same in each case. Never mind that Reform and Orthodoxy emerged in nineteenth-century Germany, and that Shiism and Sunnism emerged in ninth-century Baghdad. In the hands of a bad comparitivist, they are imagined as comparable to one another.

Another example comes by way of Nathan C. Funk and Meena Sharify Funk who write in their essay "Peacemaking Among the Children of Abraham," which appeared in an edited volume with the title *The Meeting of Civilizations* edited by Moshe Ma'oz (2009), that

> Given the extent to which Abrahamic religions have been coopted by religious nationalism and drawn into contemporary geopolitical conflict, building Abrahamic solidarity will require sustained efforts to challenge the legitimacy of religious as well as secular militancy, and to transform the role of religion in conflict by providing positive options. (Funk and Funk 2009: 214)

Again, and this is one of the hallmarks of this ecumenical literature, history is largely overlooked. The three ("Abrahamic") religions are believed to be, at root, identical to one another, and the main reason there is conflict between them is because of "non-religious" forces (e.g., politics, culture) that have nothing to do with the sacred centers of each tradition. In fact, these sacred centers, existing far from the light of politics, history, economics, and so on, represent "real" or "authentic" religious expression. In fact, it is history that seems to be the problem. Eliade, for example, regularly warned against the "terrors of history," which he imagined as the linear march of events, which by their very nature, are devoid of any inherent value or sacrality.

Whither?

Whether polemical or ecumenical, the history and ultimate goals of comparison surveyed in this chapter have been relatively similar. Be it the demonstration of ontological difference or the perception of a sacred essence behind apparently discrete expressions, comparison has been and continues to be a dubious enterprise to explicate a set of conclusions to which one has assented before the activity has even begun. The comparison then precedes as if it is the most natural thing in the world and the comparativist is simply bringing a number of self-evident truths to light. There is very little self-reflection and even less desire to establish for oneself and one's readers what the geographical and historical parameters should be. Left unanswered, because unasked, are why, what, when, and how one is comparing in the first place.

Whether to show difference or to maintain similarity, the method is often the same: to remove religions from the light of history and to reduce them to oversimplified reifications of themselves—often in ways that neatly suit the comparative project or agenda of the comparativist—with the aim of putting them in faulty and often anachronistic juxtaposition. Comparison then takes place using a set of generalizations that even schoolboys should be embarrassed to use: "Islam," the "Muslim mind," "Islamic consciousness," and so on and so forth. The results are, for the most part, absolutely meaningless and impossible to submit to any kind of independent verification. If comparison served as a role in the creation and maintenance of orthodoxy in the premodern period, more modern forms have been equally problematic. Now, removed from history and reduced to an essence, comparison pretends to be an objective enterprise, but is often anything but.

An important set of questions that we must now confront are: Will it be possible to rescue comparison from its messy and often highly partisan past in order to, if not actually reclaim, then at the very least appreciate what it *might* be able to do under properly controlled parameters? Is comparison little more than a subjective term that is invoked in order to give a highly problematic activity a semblance of scientific objectivity? Can there ever be a truly comparative study?

The Third Term

One possible solution to this conundrum is suggested by J. Z. Smith, one of the few scholars who has reflected more on comparison than anyone else in our field in recent years. Wary of the fact that too often comparison has been used phenomenologically to privilege certain religious expressions over others, he argues that every comparison (x is like y) implies, but rarely receives, a third term (with respect to z).[2] This means that, for Smith, comparison is not based on natural affinity or even historical process, but personal utility. We must remember and duly acknowledge that it is we who are the ones making the comparison and the idiosyncratic nature of this activity produces artificial if heuristically useful results. Comparison is, again in the words of Smith,

> a disciplined exaggeration in the service of knowledge. It lifts out and strongly marks certain features within difference as being of possible intellectual significance, expressed in the rhetoric of their being "like" in some stipulated fashion. Comparison provides the means by which we "revision" phenomena as *our* data in order to solve *our* theoretical problems. (Smith 1990: 52)

For Smith, "the statement of comparison is never dyadic, but always triadic; there is always an implicit 'more than,' and there is always a 'with respect to.' In the case of an academic comparison, the 'with respect to' is most frequently the scholar's interest, be this expressed in a question, a theory, or a model" (*ibid*.: 51).

This is certainly an important feature, and it would seem to cut down on the often implicit agenda that tend to govern comparative religion. Also worth noting is the fact that Smith never engages in massive and grandiose comparative projects. He looks at specific times and places—for example, late antique Jerusalem—to probe a specific question (e.g., how various social actors map space as "sacred"). Note that he is not interested, as Eliade was, in the sacred, but in how human communities make meaning for themselves often by sublimating certain discourses as divine.

"Jew" and "Muslim": An Example

The academic study of religion, as we have just seen, is a field littered with suppressed third terms, self-serving differentials, and hidden meanings.[3] Let me take up an example from my own area of research in order to underscore further just how problematic comparison has been. In his *Jews and Muslims*, Shlomo Dov Goitein, one of the pioneers in research into the Cairo Genizah,[4] coined the term "symbiosis" to refer to the historical interaction between Jews and Muslims, Judaism and Islam.[5] The basic narrative that "symbiosis" structures goes something like this: Judaism helped to give birth to Islam in the late sixth century before Islam returned the favor in the tenth to twelfth centuries by facilitating the rise and florescence of, among other things, Hebrew belles-lettres and Jewish philosophy. Informing this dominant narrative is the fiction of a creative and stable and monolithic Jewish essence that gives life to Islam (as it had to Christianity several centuries earlier) and that later borrows from a now equally creative and stable Islam what it needs. Both essences are assumed to remain untouched by this encounter. While others have tried to modify this somewhat (e.g., Laskier and Lev 2011a, 2011b), "symbiosis" is still largely our default metaphor (Wasserstrom 1995).

Goitein, it seems, was attracted to the concept of "symbiosis" because it facilitated a conceptual framework that preserved Judaism's unique features, its ahistorical essence, within a dominant culture while still enabling Jews to be full participants within it. Islam, for him, was "from the very flesh and bone of Judaism" (Goitein 1955: 130). Or, again: "Judaism could draw freely and copiously from Muslim civilization and, at the same time, preserve its independence and integrity far more completely than it was able to do in the modern world or in the Hellenistic society of Alexandria" (*ibid.*).

Goitein, and this is a hallmark of comparison, makes one of his comparanda, Judaism, into something stable, already articulated, and well defined in the sixth-century Hijaz (i.e., the western part of the Arabian Peninsula and the home to Mecca and Medina). This conceit sustains the basic and still largely regnant model wherein Jews shape Islam, and the Qur'an simply recycles midrashim and other Jewish literature of the period. It is a model, however, that always assumes that the influence moves in one direction. Left unasked are a series of important *historical* questions:

- Who were these "Jews"?
- What did "Jew" signify" in sixth-century Arabia?

We have to be cautious of assuming an orthodoxy of stable Jewish identity and practice based upon what the rabbinic academies of Babylonia were producing at this time. What "Arab Jewishness" consisted of, in other words, might have looked considerably different from other forms of Jewishness in the larger context of the Mediterranean basin.

In this one example we witness a rather traditional description of how comparison has been used: to protect, to assign value, and ultimately to envisage a desired normativity. Religions, here imagined as species or organisms, interact with one another in such a manner that one of them, Judaism, is stable, and this stability permits it to transfer its essence of monotheism to the framers of Islam. Judaism gives, Islam receives. A couple of centuries later, Islam returns the favor, but this return in no way impacts Judaism's eternal core. Changes in the latter context are superficial or cosmetic at best, and in no way transform what Judaism is or is meant to be.

When done in such an overhanded manner, comparison is completely unhelpful as an analytical method. It tells us nothing that we do not already suspect. It confirms hunches. And it supplies a convenient narrative that reinforces half-truths. The traditional use of comparison, in short, does little to make us uncomfortable precisely because it refuses to destabilize our understanding of "religion." As a model, comparison tends to work on the assumption that religions are "things" that can be reified, disembodied, removed from distinct social contexts, and assumed to interact symbiotically. The results are all around us: twelfth-century textual expressions can be compared to fourth-century ones, and not infrequently in ways that exist not just temporally, but also spatially or geographically far apart from one another.

Yet this is why, at least on one level, Goitein's model of symbiosis is potentially interesting. He is interested in specific contexts among two religions that we know interacted historically, religiously, intellectually, socially, and economically with one another. There is perhaps no greater testament to this than his six-volume *A Mediterranean Society*, which documents the historical interactions between two local communities, including at the familial and individual level. However, when it comes to speaking about religion, Goitein neither theorizes religion nor is he particularly interested in it.[6] It just seems to be there, amorphously and silently informing the inner lives of those he studies through their written texts and correspondences.

But just because Goitein's model, like the models of so many in our field, is faulty does not necessarily mean that we have to jettison certain aspects of the comparative enterprise. Rather than see two separate and fully defined species interact, why not start with the fact—and it is a fact since we have absolutely no idea who the Jews of the sixth-century Arabian Peninsula were or what they subscribed to when it came to doctrine—that two proximate social groups developed in tandem with one another and used a common structure and vocabulary. What would eventually become two distinct and discrete religions—Judaism and Islam—took considerable time to coalesce in such a manner that each gained definition from, with, and by the other. What is decidedly not the case, and this is the assumption of many who reproduce the "symbiosis" thesis, is the interaction of two fully developed religions that, although sharing certain superficial phenomena (language, literature), retained their separate essences.

In the next chapter I wish to examine some possible ways that we might rehabilitate comparison. This will then set the stage for a larger discussion of some of the possibilities that comparison way well offer us in the academic study of religion.

Notes

1. Important exceptions include McCutcheon (1997: 27–50), Strenski (1987), and Dubuisson ([1993]2006).
2. See his discussion in Smith (1990: 50–53).
3. This section is drawn from and reworks Hughes (2017).
4. The Cairo Genizah is a collection of some 300,000 Jewish and some Muslim manuscript fragments that were found in the storeroom of a synagogue in

Old Cairo, Egypt. They represent a roughly 1,000-year continuum (870 CE to nineteenth century) of Jewish–Muslim and Judeo-Arabic history and comprise a diverse collection of medieval manuscripts—everything from tax receipts and personal letters to biblical manuscripts.
5. And subsequently recycled by the likes of Bernard Lewis (1984: xi, 191) and Sarah Stroumsa (2011: 3–6).
6. In his "Religion in Everyday Life as Reflected in the Documents of the Cairo Genizah," one of the first collections supported and produced by the newly formed Association for Jewish Studies, Goitein writes:

> The religion of the Genizah people was a stern, straightforward, Talmudic type of piety; concerned with the strict fulfillment of the commandments and with the pursuit of study required for their knowledge. This somewhat jejune character of their religiosity was enhanced by the rigorous rationalism embraced by Jewish orthodoxy in the wake of centuries of sectarian and theological controversies. (Goitein 1974: 8)

Chapter 3

Possibilities

If the previous chapter witnessed some of the historical uses and abuses to which the comparative method, if in fact we can call what passed for it a method, has been put, the present chapter seeks to confront such abuses and begin the process of reclaiming comparison for more sober-minded and analytical purposes. If comparison is to be rehabilitated, it is necessary to remove it from the hands of apologists who seek to insulate their own chosen concept or religion using the guise of scientific objectivity. In like manner, comparison must also avoid the often equally apologetic language of influence and borrowing. If the former represents the complacency of the scholar of religion, it is the latter—the search for who had what first—that is frequently the conceit of the historian. It is now time to begin the process of transforming comparison into something rigorous and systematic, a method that can account for the dynamics of social groups, including their interactions, and the ways in which they change based on such interactions. This is not an easy task, however. It means walking a tortuous path between a self-consciousness of why one is comparing in the first place and an academic honesty that is sustained by the notion that conclusions cannot be predetermined.

In his *Drudgery Divine*, Jonathan Z. Smith provides us with one of his many cautions when undertaking comparison. Using the overlap between early Christianity and late Second Temple Judaisms as his dataset, he shows with typical acumen and clarity how such comparisons have traditionally been done for many non-scholarly reasons, despite appeals to the contrary. As is so common in religious studies, personal or extra-scholarly agendas masquerade as scholarly endeavors. Although such motives and motivations should be obvious, however, those engaging in such dubious comparisons, as we have seen, have no problems invoking equivocal terms like "science" or "objectivity." "Thus the issue of comparing words," Smith writes, "has never been primarily a philological issue, but always an apologetic one" (1990: 83). The often technical and scientific discipline of philology, in other words, provides the ostensible cover for various nefarious activities. Just as philology is invoked for a set of extra-philological agendas, we frequently see history invoked for a set of equally extra- or trans-historical goals.

As with the previous chapter, however, it is still necessary to put a more responsible comparative approach in direct counterpoint with what I imagine to be highly problematic contemporary uses. Before I do this, however, it is necessary to step back momentarily and talk positively about some of the features of comparison and just what it can bring to an analysis, *when done properly*. My main argument, to reiterate, is that comparison ought not to be a global method, that is, something that compares and contrasts the religions of the globe in an essentialized fashion. It is, on the contrary, something that can be useful only when employed sparingly, cautiously, and with a certain trepidation that is one of the hallmarks of scholarly self-reflexivity. No self-respecting scholar can now be so bold as to compare whole religions because, as should now be evident to even the beginning student, religions are not monolithic entities. There is, appeals to the contrary, no "Jewish" take on the world; neither is there a "Buddhist" mindset, a "Hindu" consciousness, or a "Christian" genius. There are, however, social groups that appeal to the rhetoric supplied by religion (that is, a set of discourses that they somehow regard as transcendent). Our job is not to compare the religious "truths" of these groups writ large, but the social meanings that localized and contextually specific groups create for themselves.

Perhaps reflective of this, recent years have seen a growing tendency in the field to speak of religions as opposed to religion or Buddhisms instead of Buddhism (i.e., using the plural as opposed to the singular form of these nouns). Within this context, however, Arnal and McCutcheon are correct to note that "the erstwhile singular family identity in each case is just deferred to the level of genus; identity of some sort remains intact, unspoken, and thus untheorized" (Arnal and McCutcheon 2013: 11-12). So, despite the tendency to speak in plurals and the concomitant desire to problematize identity, the two—that is, a monolithic religion and a stable identity—are often left standing at the end of comparative analyses. Yet the goal of comparison ought to be to undermine or destabilize identity not further reinscribe it. Comparison, then, has to be able to appreciate and account for this instability. If not, it becomes a method that simply replicates what one considers to be the self-evident and the status quo—this is something that comparison is in danger of becoming if it has not largely become that already, and this is the main reason that many are increasingly mistrustful of the term and/or method. Comparison, then, has to systematically rethink the inherited order and the ways that we are accustomed to speak about the intersection of identities that are often sublimated and rationalized by appeals to religion. The goal of comparison is to try to unravel all of these identities and show how related and/or contiguous social groups interact among themselves and with others, and often in ways that are similar in response to social and political stimuli. Comparison ought not to work with discrete identities that bump against one another while largely remaining intact, but should instead be able to account for overlapping identities that are perceived to represent the complexity of social formation.

Too often comparison works on a model of discrete identities and, in so doing, employs—whether consciously or unconsciously—one of two models. The first is that while putative interactions may occur between groups, identity is rarely challenged in the interaction. This is the "symbiotic" model we saw at the end of the previous chapter, and one I shall discuss in greater detail below. The second, the "phenomenological," is even less specific and compares x in one tradition with y in another, often with little or no attention to geographic or temporal contexts. Much of this chapter is concerned with the first type of comparison and with how to find a new vocabulary that can ideally permit more analytically useful types of comparison and, in the process, facilitate a way to talk about the historical and social connections between religions in a nuanced manner. The payoff of such an approach is great: even though we all ostensibly work in specific religious traditions that imply their own set of linguistic and historical training, if we do our jobs properly, then others engaged in the academic study of religion and who work on similar problems, albeit in different temporal and geographical contexts, will hopefully find our own limited endeavors to be of some value.

Comparison enables us to envisage an issue or a problem (though, again, one largely of our own imagining) in our own dataset and reveals it as a larger issue relevant to human worldmaking. In this it is fundamentally unlike area studies, which tend to work in parochial areas relevant to particular geographic areas (e.g., African American studies, Middle Eastern studies, Jewish studies) and, in the process, often reifies notions of ethnic and/or racial identity and, not infrequently, engages in special pleading. Unfortunately, the academic study of religion is constantly under threat from becoming little more than a canopy—a "big tent" to use the locution of the American Academy of Religion (AAR)—under which cohabit a variety of area studies and their concomitant identity politics (see Hughes 2015a). Comparison, however, ought to show us that nothing is unique. Different social groups—and it is under this rubric that we must ultimately put *specific and historically contingent* groups who make appeals to religion or some other transcendently signified discourse—make meaning for themselves in ways that reveal similar (but *not* the same) features. However, we can admit that under properly controlled conditions it is possible to make certain small-c comparisons betwixt and between such groups as opposed to some grand, capital-C Comparison.

Comparison thus permits the articulation of a problem using technical and non-participant language, and simultaneously shows how certain ideas or items—understood as social factoids—may be similar (but not identical) to the ways in which other social groups make meaning. Mistakes arise when we want to replace "social groups" with "religions." The latter implies that there is some specific Muslim (or Jewish or any other religious) way of engaging the world, one that exists beyond specific temporal or geographical locations. If we avoid such gross generalizations and essentializations, it can be possible to examine how social groups make sense of their world and how they do so in ways that are distinctly mundane and quotidian.

Words and Narratives

Although comparison may be a cognitive act (see, for example, Paden 2016), it takes place in narratives and does so, moreover, using language. Both of these are necessarily grounded in metaphors that, according to Lakoff and Johnson, are not mere poetic indulgences, but actually structure our perceptions and understanding of reality (Lakoff and Johnson 1980: 3–6). The words we choose, the narratives we decide on, framed somewhat differently, construct our objects of study as opposed to vice versa. For this reason, it is incumbent upon us to analyze and understand these narratives since they are largely responsible for putting various and diverse religious forms and expressions in counterpoint, for describing their interaction with one another, and ultimately for reproducing certain agendas about what religions are or should be. The majority of our default models work on the assumption that religions are comprised of eternal and timeless essences that—despite the fact that they may undergo spatial, temporal, and geographical manifestation—remain beyond the pale of history. Let me use the example of Judaism. Often imagined underpinning all Jewish expressions—from, say, Second Temple Alexandria to Cordoba in Muslim Spain to early Modern Venice to nineteenth-century Vilnius to modern-day Crown Heights or Tel Aviv—is some amorphous sense of "Jewishness." Larger contexts are all but ignored, non-normative groups that do not fit a model of what Judaism should be are marginalized or written out, and the overwhelming assumption is that there is some golden chain that links diverse and disparate Jews into a neat and tidy model that focuses on a few variables (e.g., observance of *halakhah* or Jewish law).

Such a model, however, ignores the fact that each one of the communities listed in the previous paragraph possessed its own set of concerns that, in turn, were responsible for structuring their understanding not only of Judaism but of themselves. Certainly *halakhic* observance may have been one such concern, but it is by no means the only one nor even the most important. We do a disservice to each of these communities when we make claims to the contrary, and in the process lose sight of all those social and other cultural factors that went into and indeed continue to go into the creation of community.

Even on the level of language—Second Temple Jews were Aramaic or Greek speakers, Cordoban Jews were Arabic speakers, and the Jews of Vilnius were, for the most part, Yiddish speaking—each one of these communities understood themselves in light of the larger linguistic and other cultural contexts in which they lived. So while some might want to compare Jews across time and geography to get at some inchoate sense of "Jewishness," perhaps more valid comparisons might well take place between social groups that define themselves as Jews and those that do not in specific times and places (e.g., Wasserstrom 1995; Bodian 1999; Boyarin 2014; Hughes 2017) with respect, for example, to a third term.

A negative example should suffice for the purpose of illustration. In his *God is Not One*, Stephen Prothero, as his subtitle makes clear, is interested in comparing "the religions that run the world." Seemingly writing for a largely uninformed audience, his goal is to show how religions do not share the same essence, but that the "world's religious rivals are clearly related, but they are more like second cousins than identical twins" (Prothero 2010: 13). While the first goal (that religions do not share the same essence) is certainly correct, he does not make the logical second move, which would be to argue that even groups within religions do not share the same essence. Unfortunately, however, he does not do this. Instead his goal is to illumine for his general readership that we need to understand religions in order to understand the world's problems: "It is impossible to understand politics in India and the economy of China without knowing something about Hinduism and Confucianism" (*ibid.*: 11). In many ways this is self-serving. The world needs scholars of religion because they are the only ones who can penetrate beyond the surface and understand the entire worldview of religions. If you want to understand banking practices in India, become a Religious Studies major and learn about Hinduism. This, of course, is ludicrous. About what Hinduism is Prothero speaking? Is it the Hinduism, say, of the time of the Buddha, of today, or of some time in between? Also overlooked is the very Western construction or invention of Hinduism (see, e.g., King 1999; Pennington 2005). Does understanding Confucianism, as Prothero believes, help us better understand the political and martial culture of China? Certainly not. Prothero, then, works with a naïve and oversimplified notion of religion: that it structures thinking as opposed to vice versa. The religions of the globe, for Prothero, are simplistically and monolithically assumed to be synonymous with a particular worldview that cannot be reduced to politics, social formation, or ideology. In order to get at this worldview he comes up with a model, into which he situates his eight world-running rival religions. Each religion is based on:

- a *problem*;
- a *solution* to this problem, which also serves as the religious goal;
- a *technique* (or techniques) for moving from this problem to this solution; and
- an *exemplar* (or exemplars) who chart this path from problem to solution (Prothero 2010: 14).

An example should suffice. In Christianity, at least for Prothero, the problem is sin; the solution is salvation; the technique is faith and good works; and the exemplars are saints in Catholicism and ordinary people of faith in Protestantism (*ibid.*: 14). And, with this model, we thereby understand Christianity and presumably something of American politics (*ibid.*: 11). That is it. There is little or no nuance. A religion can be reduced to a few slogans or sound bites with no appreciation of historical, textual, or geographical diversity.

Prothero's model, I would suggest, offers us the worst possible one for engaging in comparison at the current moment. Each religion (note the singular) articulates a different, but related, problem, and seeks to solve it in different ways. While his goal is to show the diversity among the world's religions, he unfortunately provides none *within* each religion. The result is a superficial presentation that hinders actual analysis instead of helping it.

One negative example deserves a positive one that can hopefully replace it. Within this latter context a pertinent example comes by way of J. Z. Smith's *To Take Place* (1987), a work that, while interested in localized and contextualized comparison, draws upon other examples to illumine his particular dataset. In this work Smith seeks to understand a general and universal question that relates to how humans make meanings: how place, in particular constructed ritual environments, structure and sanctify particular actions as rituals. To get at this larger question he focuses on a particular example that is based on his own linguistic and historical training in Second Temple Judaism. Within this context, he focuses specifically on the Temple envisioned by the prophet Ezekiel in the biblical book that bears his name and the Church of the Holy Sepulcher. In order to show that his data is not unique, however, and to show how it can be illumined by other data, he *moves out* from late antique Judaism to read the work of others who engage similar problems of space, urbanization, and ritual. Smith, for example, argues that the writings of Paul Wheatley, who works on the ancient Chinese city, provide us with

> a range of terminology and notions on which we will continue to draw: the city as a "ceremonial center" with one of its chief crafts being the "technology of ritual display"; the city as an "organizing principle"; and urbanism as the "hierarchical patterning of society in its totality." (Smith 1987: 52)

Smith's goal here is not to show that space/ritual is the same all over the globe or that it somehow permits us to understand better Jewish or Christian banking practices (à la Prothero), but instead to reveal that scholars working on a similar problem but with different datasets can actually aid those working in different traditions. In addition to Wheatley, he examines the work of Clifford Geertz and Louis Dumont. The former provides him with the language to examine the topic of hierarchy and social differentiation, whereas the latter distinguishes between systems of status and systems of power (*ibid.*: 54). "Drawing on what we have learned from Wheatley, Geertz and Dumont," Smith writes, "we may return to the text of Ezekiel" (*ibid.*: 56). Smith, in other words, starts with a problem, moves out to look how said problem is examined by experts working in other traditions and/or disciplines, and then returns to his own data that can now be illumined, but not elided, by the exercise. Comparison, on this model, is about finding an adequate theoretical vocabulary to account for one's data. This is a far cry from the claims of Joseph Campbell and Mircea Eliade with which I began this volume. These two individuals, and many others who have followed in their wake, were interesting in sweeping aside all historical and social contexts to arrive at some sort of self-proclaimed deep meaning. I take a much more critical (or even cynical) approach and maintain that there are no "deep meanings" only richly textured contexts.

But also note what Smith is *not* doing. He is not interested in looking for a one-size-fits-all paradigm to explain the intersectionality of place and ritual. Nor is he attempting to locate the sacred though its spatial morphology. Instead, since Smith does not know the languages of ancient China or those of the tribes of Bali, he examines the work of those who do. His goal is not to show similarity, but difference—or, perhaps better, a difference that is inflected by a similar question or set of questions. Smith's attention to detail, his unwillingness to assume that difference is secondary to some presumed essence that awaits detection, in addition to his emphasis that scholarship is always an act of choice, selection, and focus, offers a much different and more nuanced model than the one offered by Prothero above.

I agree with the likes of Smith, who argue that cross-cultural comparisons are of limited value except to draw attention to one's own dataset. Since many of us do not know all the languages of the globe (both ancient and modern), any comparison that attempts to work with religious texts in translation will prove to be problematic, some might say even impossible. It means, for example, that we must rely on the translations and ultimately biases of others. Furthermore, it means that we have largely used these texts as if they somehow exist as timeless artifacts regardless of social or historical provenance.

Let me illustrate this with another example. I formerly edited a book series with Oxford University Press and I still recall a glaring problem with one of the first submissions to my series—though I did not realize it at the time since I do not work in this particular area. The author in question desired to engage in a comparative study of Asian fire rituals based not on their formal characteristics (which might have been fine at least for an AAR book series), but instead on specific rituals called *"homa."* This author's entire thesis was predicated on the "fact" that the *homa* rituals encountered across Asia, and which are generally assumed to derive from Indic prototypes, actually came from an Iranian/Zoroastrian model in the Avestan language. The key piece of evidence for this author was that the Avestan word *haoma* was the equivalent to the Sanskrit *homa*, and that there was a (Proto-)Indo-Iranian, pre-Vedic word *homa* underlying both the Avestan and the Iranian fire rituals. When I sent the manuscript out for review, I did what I always do: I sent it to a religionist working in the area and to an expert in the same area but not in religious studies. In this case, the religionist loved it, but the specialist informed me that the manuscript was based on a fundamental error, namely, that the Avestan *haoma* could never be cognate to Sanskrit *homa* since the former was instead a direct cognate to Sanskrit *soma*, both deriving from the Proto-Indo-Iranian **sauma*. If Avestan did have a cognate to Sanskrit *homa*, my expert reader informed me, it would be **zauma*, which does not exist (or at least is not attested). The anonymous reviewer concluded that "The whole work is based on a fundamental – and embarrassingly elementary – error, and the author seems not to know any of the languages and textual sources on which his/her work rests."

This rather technical example offers a stunning example of the danger of comparison, at least in the academic study of religion. It would *seem* to be based on a knowledge of the languages and contexts of the data in question, but it appears—when confronted by a specialist in the actual area—to be completely faulty. This is why comparison *must* involve a proper understanding of texts and contexts, theory and history. In the case of our anonymous comparativist, she should have written a work—although whether or not she had the requisite textual and historical skills is uncertain—in such a manner that would have appealed to both of the readers to whom the manuscript was sent.

To return us to the theme of this section: it is necessary to pay attention to the words that we use to imagine religions in counterpoint, just as it is essential that we pay sufficient attention to the narratives that such words structure, facilitate, and ultimately disseminate. In the following section I wish to examine one such narrative that has largely ordered our historical understanding of the relationship between Jews and Muslims. I wish to show that despite appeals to history, this narrative is in fact anything but historical. If anything, these narratives predispose us to think about their interactions in a particular way and often in such a manner that it is difficult to move beyond this particular way of thinking. This is the danger: comparisons often come with built-in narratives that make it difficult to begin afresh and that prevent or discourage us from looking at datasets that involve comparanda in new ways.

Judaism and Islam: A Case Study in Narrative

There exists a traditional narrative that structures our understanding of the "historical" relations between Jews and Muslims.[1] We encountered this narrative at the end of the previous chapter, and it runs something like the following: Judaism functioned as a midwife to Islam in the late sixth century by providing it with the monotheistic wherewithal needed for its survival before Islam returned the favor in the tenth to twelfth centuries by facilitating the rise and florescence of, among other things, Hebrew literature and Jewish rationalism.

Using this example, allow me to reflect upon comparison more specifically. This narrative implies:

- that a fully normative and rabbinic Judaism created Islam—though of course we are never told how, just that it happened; and
- that several centuries later, the Jewish contact with Islam allowed Jews to express themselves using new literary forms and genres that they inherited from Muslims.

Informing this dominant narrative is the fiction of a creative and stable Jewish essence that gives life to Islam (as it had to Christianity several centuries earlier) and that later subsequently borrows from a now equally creative and stable Islam what it needs. Much intellectual labor has gone on in the modern period to examine the latter. Unfortunately such a model retells a set of platitudes that many, scholars included, assumed happened. Left unasked are a series of difficult questions:

- Who, for example, were "the Jews" with whom Muhammad interacted (i.e., who is to say that they were normative or rabbinic)?

- How exactly did Judaism transform during the so-called "golden age" (i.e., did its essence change or was the change simply superficial)?
- What exactly happened to the Jews between these chronological bookends?

The metaphor most invoked to describe this interrelationship is "symbiosis," which, as we witnessed in the previous chapter, was originally coined in the 1950s, though it had been implicit for decades prior to this. A decent comparative framework, however, ought to theorize the terms bequeathed to us since such terms ultimately structure our entire narrative. Symbiosis is a metaphor derived from the field of biology, and it is used in that field to describe the mutually beneficial relationship between two or more species or organisms. Judaism and Islam, using this narrative, are imagined as two distinct "species" whose borders would seem to touch in such a manner that their centers, their perceived internal cores of stability and essence, remain untainted by the exchange. Exchange, in other words, is structured as largely superficial, with each "species" nudging the other along at a formative moment of its "evolution" (if we retain the semantic grid of biology). No fluidity is posited as each species partakes of its own concerns specific to its own set of organisms. Implicit in the metaphor is that Judaism and Islam need one another and that each has depended on the other for its existence—this is a romantic or wistful claim, however, and not a biological one. It is at this point that we see their conflation. Although Goitein never theorized "symbiosis," we can and, moreover, it is incumbent upon us to do so in order to ascertain what, if any, categorical or other problems may lurk in the background.

There are at least three different types of symbiotic relationships: *mutualism*, where both the symbiont and host, or the two symbionts, benefit; *commensalism*, where the symbiont benefits with little effect on the host; and *parasitism*, where the symbiont benefits to the detriment of the host. What does "symbiosis" allow Goitein to do? Since he neither problematizes nor theorizes the term, it seems to just exist for him naturally in the world, and it does so, moreover, in a manner that implies "mutualism," that is, a *mutually beneficial* relationship between the symbiont and the host. There are certainly other biological metaphors he could have used, like evolution or co-evolution, if in fact religions evolve or history is teleological. Although symbiosis is certainly the predominant narrative, it has engendered others. One such example is "commensalism" (see Laskier and Lev 2011a), which, as we have just seen, is one type of symbiosis, namely, a type of relationship between two organisms where only one organism benefits without affecting the other. The organism that does not benefit is presumably neutral. This means that while Judaism benefitted Islam by gifting the latter its monotheistic content, Judaism remained unscathed by the relationship. Sociologically, however, "commensality" refers to the practice of eating together, something that definitely has irenic or, "idyllic" overtones, and is related to the notion of *convivencia*, a term with equally irenic and interfaith overtones (see Menocal 2003).[2]

Laskier and Lev (2011b) have also edited a companion volume, *The Divergence of Judaism and Islam*, which would seem to imply a different metaphoric orientation. Again, though, they are largely uninterested in the semantic fallout of their choice of metaphors. Presumably they invoke the trope of "divergence" as the opposite of their previous volume's "convergence," and as a way to signal the so-called "parting of the ways" between Judaism and Islam after a certain period that, for them, is tantamount to "the end of the nineteenth century to the onset of the third millennium" (*ibid*.: 1). They fail to note, though, that if they are going to use metaphors to describe a comparative relationship between two species/religions, they have to tell us what sort of intellectual work it purports to do or, at the very least, they need to show both the heuristic utility and/or cognitive relevance of transcribing a biological metaphor onto a religious studies register. In biology, for example, genetic divergence is used to speak of ancestral species that develop genetic mutations independent of one another across time, after they have become isolated from one another. In ophthalmology, to use another example, "divergence" signifies the simultaneous outward movement of both eyes away from each other, with the aim of maintaining single binocular vision when viewing an object. If we followed through with what the metaphor implies, they would seem to suggest that the two religions move away from one another involuntarily in order that they may create a single and better vision.

Laskier and Lev show us the consequences when we do not think through the semantic range of meanings of the words and narratives that we choose to describe the relations between religions. Our language, to reiterate, does not naturally describe facts on the ground, but simultaneously structures and processes the "facts" that we want to see. When we use metaphors derived from the realm of biology and then transfer them to another field of study there is bound to be semantic fallout. Religions are not biological species and when we name them as such we make them into something they are not.

When we repeat the narrative of symbiosis, and it is indeed repeated with some degree of regularity,[3] we invoke both a way of talking about religions (i.e., as species) and of comparison (i.e., rarely more than skin deep). This narrative, to reiterate, actively creates the religions it seeks to examine, and how, when, and why they interact with one another. Judaism, for so many who work on this material, now becomes the normative rabbinic Judaism of later centuries, a stable religious system that provides the epistemic content and vocabulary for Muhammad and his early followers. Ignoring the obvious Orientalist themes of such a narrative—Judaism (and, of course, Christianity) as active and thus masculine, and Islam as passive and therefore feminine—it overlooks the fact that we know absolutely nothing about the Jews, if in fact they were Jews or just a later projection, who lived on the Arabian Peninsula at the time of Muhammad. We do not possess, for example, a *miqva* (a ritual bath), an ossuary, let alone a cemetery or other archeological features and/or structures that would suggest a Jewish presence in the area. Certainly later sources tell us of Jewish tribes in the area, but we have no idea what these Jews believed, practiced, wrote, or thought. We have absolutely no idea what their relationship was to the Jews of Jerusalem, Babylonia, or other centers. They may well have been Arab tribes that considered themselves to be somehow Jewish—keeping in mind that the very notions of ethnicity and religiosity are modern constructs—who otherwise differed very little, if at all, from pagan tribes.[4]

If we remove the narrative of symbiosis and instead try other possible models, a different analysis emerges. If, instead of species, we strip all theological doctrine away, we see social groups struggling to make sense of themselves and others in the light of the political instability caused by the rapid expansion of Islam in the seventh century CE. If we remove the language of who had what first or who borrowed from whom, we have less anxiety over influences and can instead attune ourselves more productively to a situation in which social groups respond to similar situations by drawing on a shared vocabulary that can be recycled in any number of ways. Comparative models, and the narratives to which they give rise, risk simplifying the data to make it fit into preexistent and often theological concerns.

Words

The words—the individual components of narratives—we choose to invoke in our efforts to compare are equally important. Again, they not only structure narratives but also govern selection of comparanda. To stay with the example in the previous section for a little longer, terms like "Judaism," "Islam," even "religion" become exceedingly difficult if not actually untenable. Religions and religious traditions do not interact, social groups composed of individuals do. These groups may invoke vocabularies that we may well signify as "religious," but if and when they do make such invocations, they are doing so for social reasons. If early proto-Muslim groups that partook of a shared late antique messianism and apocalypticism invoke a particular vocabulary, it is to make sense of their social world. If they recycle terms and motifs, it is not a conscious borrowing, but a drawing upon a collection of such motifs employed by other groups engaged in similar social construction with whom they are in contact.

Writing of the complexity of religious forms in the late antique period, Beard, North, and Price discuss the need to

> investigate the degree of religious continuity in these cults traceable across the Roman world. By and large, however, in discussing the religions of the empire we have tried to avoid thinking in terms of uniformity, or in terms of a central core "orthodox" tradition with its peripheral "variants"; we have preferred to think rather in terms

of different religions as clusters of ideas, people, and rituals, sharing some common identity across time and place, but at the same time inevitably invested with different meanings in different contexts. (Beard, North, and Price 1998: 249)

Although these scholars are speaking about the complexity of religion in the Roman Empire, their comments are certainly applicable to other geographic and social contexts. Again, I draw on the work of Beard, North, and Price as a further example to show one of the hallmarks of good comparison. Like the example from J. Z. Smith mentioned earlier, I here use the theoretical models created and developed by scholars working with different datasets but similar questions and problems. This, in turn, provides me with a theoretical vocabulary that I would otherwise not possess. When I then apply their findings to my context, my data is opened up in ways that it would not have been if I did not look outside of it. Just as I would hope that my findings would benefit them. When we examine the context of Jewish–Muslim relations—if in fact we want to call them relations because I think there was much more fluidity in play, a fluidity that is often masked by the hyphen—the data certainly supports a non-symbiotic model of comparison. The best place to look for models to help us move beyond the symbiotic approach, I submit, is to look at the messiness and complexity of social groups in the late antique period. If we do this, we might describe how nominally Jewish groups, for example, related to their messianic figures in ways more similar to how some nominally Muslim groups related to theirs than they did to other Jewish groups. This is much more useful than saying a monolithic "Judaism" gave birth to a monolithic "Islam."

In like manner some of these Jewish groups related to their body of law—or, perhaps more accurately, what was becoming their body of law—and its interpretation in ways that were phenomenally more similar to some Muslim groups than to other Jewish ones. It is this overlap that the narrative of symbiosis cannot account for. Just as it is an overlap that traditional phenomenological models completely overlook. Previous models, whether of the symbiotic or phenomenological variety, posit simplicity when the situation on the ground seems to have been much more complex. What is needed in comparative models is a systematic rethinking of not only the words that we use to invoke comparison, but, just as importantly, the narratives to which those words contribute. Once we settle on a narrative, we must then theorize it to show how it is helpful and in what cases it might be problematic. No narrative, in other words, is perfect or airtight.

Phenomenology Returns (If It Ever Left)

As we have seen repeatedly there have been two main historical reasons to engage in comparison in the academic study of religion: to show difference and to show similarity. Although both are apologetic, they have radically different ends: the former wants to make one's own religion unique and special; the latter seeks to cordon off some amorphous sense of the "sacred" that all religions are believed to share deep down. Both projects claim to be "scientific" and both claim to be value neutral. Thankfully, those studies that seek to privilege one's own religion are increasingly circumscribed in the academic study of religion and are now frequently the purview of theology—although, as we shall see shortly, they have not completely disappeared only morphed into other discourses and conversations. This, however, has not stopped a largely liberal Protestant agenda from guiding the academic study of religion, determining what counts as religion or religious and what does not (see the critique in Fitzgerald 2000).

The phenomenological approach is still alive and well in the academic study of religion. While it has certainly changed over the years, phenomenology—whether it goes by this name or not is irrelevant—remains predicated on the idea that religion is fundamentally an experiential and inner state of the individual, something that can neither be coopted by nor reduced to a host of material factors that include the political, the economic, or the social. This frequently, as we have seen, leads to a faulty comparative framework. Since all religions have some form of prayer, for example, all religions are necessarily believed to share a common notion of the sacred. Comparison, then, is the method that is continually invoked to illumine this common notion. Robert A. Orsi, in a recent essay, writes about this sacred, what he here calls the "holy," in a way that overlooks the social construction of meaning and the imposition of largely Western terms of reference,

> The holy still seems to me to name both a reality and an approach to religion that scholars of religion ought to think about. For one thing, people all over the world and in different historical periods have experienced something out of the ordinary in certain persons, places, or things, and they know what they mean, or enough of what they mean, to use the word "holy" (or one like it), even feel compelled to use it, as the only possible word for what they have experienced. This is the empirical warrant for continued interest in the term. (Orsi 2011: 85–86)

Here, Orsi seeks to make an argument as to why scholars of religion need to retain the holy. While he acknowledges that Otto's use of the term to refer to something ontologically transcendent may well be difficult to maintain in our contemporary academic climate, he nevertheless wants to retain the idea that there is something real or tangible about experiences of the holy that scholars of religion ought to acknowledge.[5] Orsi seeks to strip the material conditions away as "empirically insufficient" (*ibid.*: 84) and prefers to set "aside questions about the ontological realness of religious phenomena as a condition of research" (*ibid.*) so as to return to the experiential. He encourages scholars to see

> how Jesus is a real figure in a Pentecostal woman's everyday experience, as real to her as the other people around her, as real as her kitchen table and her arthritis. She does not "believe in" Jesus. Jesus is present to her. Moreover, this woman's Jesus has an existence that is greater than the sum of her intentions, desires, needs, hopes, and fears, and that cannot be completely accounted for with reference to her social circumstances. He has a life of his own in her life. (Orsi 2011: 84)

Historical, cultural, social, and other contexts are all swept under the proverbial carpet so that the scholar can engage in some sort of convivencia with this Pentecostal woman and her Jesus. This holy, it is assumed, is something that is present to a Jewish bar mitzvah, the Muslim shop owner, and so on. But, again, it is largely unquantifiable.

In her *Bringing the Sacred Down to Earth* (2012), Corinne G. Dempsey provides us with a model that derives its tenor from Orsi's approach. Though much more focused on comparison than Orsi, she certainly shares his interest in "lived religion."[6] Rather than invoke monolithic religions, she instead examines local interactions in specific places, and then compares these to other local contexts in other geographical contexts. On one level, then, she agrees with me that comparison has to be local and contextual; however, we depart company when she insists on still trying to locate the sacred in such contexts. She argues, for example, that comparison is primarily about "naming and claiming the sacred from different angles and a variety of settings" (*ibid.*: 5), though, as is typical of this discourse, she never names or tells us what the "sacred" actually is. It is always assumed to be unnamed. Witness, as yet another example of this approach, the relatively new book series—co-edited by Kathryn Lofton and John Lardas Modern—at the University of Chicago Press, "Class 200: New Studies in Religion." The series, in its own words,

> presumes no inaugurating definition of religion other than what it is not: it is not reducible to demographics, doctrines, or cognitive mechanics. It is more than a discursive concept or cultural idiom. *It is something that can be named only with a precise and poetic wrestling with the nature of its naming.*[7]

Returning to Dempsey, she further claims that the goal of comparison is "to shed light on angles and contours otherwise obscured within particular religious contexts and, in the process, suggest possibilities for bridging human contingencies and perceptions across religious, cultural, and disciplinary divides" (Dempsey 2012: 5). While aware of comparison's potential to reify and abstract, including its historical use in privileging certain forms over others, Dempsey contends that the way to overcome such pitfalls is "the resolve to take seriously the religious experiences and expressions of those we study" (*ibid.*: 10). Since we have no access to the inner experiences of others, we must "take seriously" that which they tell us. The hermeneutics of suspicion, reductionism, and a certain cynicism—all hallmarks of sober and critical scholarship in most academic disciplines—are here largely dismissed and replaced by some form of naïve color-commentary.

For Dempsey, comparison is contemporary and not textual. She primarily deals with localized traditions supplied by South Asian and Euro-american contexts (e.g., Indian neo-Vedanta and Icelandic spiritualism, or Indian and Irish Catholicism). What makes comparison possible for Dempsey is the illusive nature of the sacred, something that, according to her, functions "as a category that implies ties to transcendent meaning and power yet is not limited to or divided against the unempirical or the metaphysical" (*ibid.*: 15). This would seem to be a variation on the theme of Eliade that hierophanies "revert to an archetype." Comparison, in other words, allows us to get at the sacred just as the sacred facilitates comparison. This circle, however, ultimately reproduces and reifies what it seeks to discover in the first place. Dempsey's notion of comparison thus takes us back to an earlier time in its deployment. The sacred, once again, is the business of the scholar of religion, whose charge and *raison d'être* is to reveal it in all its ethereal and nonempirical complexity.

This neo-phenomenological approach, while seemingly more attentive to context, nevertheless continues to pivot unsuccessfully around something vague and amorphous. A question those of us interested in comparison and non-phenomenological approaches might ask ourselves is: what might Demspey's comparison look like without appeals to transcendent meaning? If she removed talk of the sacred and instead replaced it with comparative notions of social facts and worldmaking, what would her analysis gain?

Uniqueness Redux

If phenomenology has never left, it seems that its nemesis, namely, comparison to show how one's own religion is unique, still lurks uncomfortably in the background.[8] In his *Created Equal*, Joshua A. Berman (2008) seeks to demonstrate, as the subtitle of his book makes clear, how the Bible "broke with ancient political thought." When anything "breaks from" something else, an apologetic agenda is often not that far away from the surface. Since neither ancient Israel nor its neighbors had the term or the category "political," taxonomic and ontological uniqueness is extremely problematic to determine if it is to be based on a set of terms that lie outside the scope of ancient Near Eastern political thought. How, framed somewhat differently, can the religious traditions of ancient Israel break with that of its neighbors over anachronistic terms and categories?

In order to produce such a reading, however, Berman has to remove the Bible from its Near Eastern context and show how it either anticipates or influences—both extremely problematic words in the history of ideas—some of the great ideas in Western political thought, from Machiavelli and Hobbes to those who created the American Constitution. Whereas other Near Eastern texts are products of their times, thereby reproducing divine rights of kings, class-based societies, and fickle gods, the Bible hovers above such texts presumably on account of its eternal message of equality. An example of this should suffice for the present: "Scanning theories from Roman jurists through Montesquieu," he writes in his Introduction, "I conclude that the kernel of a theory of [governmental] checks and balances that one may adduce from a reading of Deuteronomy is suggestive of formulations we do not encounter again until the writings of the American founding fathers" (Berman 2008: 10). Biblical exceptionalism, on his reading, leads into American exceptionalism. Just as ancient Israel broke with the monarchical despotisms of its neighbors, it is implied, America did the same with its European cousins.

Although ancient Greek theorists were not truly egalitarian, according to Berman, because they only took into consideration a select body of males, he is willing to overlook the exclusion of women from the ancient Israelite polity. While he acknowledges this exclusion, he nevertheless implies that it may not actually have been such, since "at some junctures, as in the collective address of the entire polity (second person plural 'you'), it *may* be that men and women are addressed in equal fashion" (*ibid.*: 13; my italics; see the criticisms in Ackerman 2010). Berman simply refuses to consider that the egalitarianism that he sees reflected in the Bible can just as easily be described as religious absolutism. Later in the book, he seems to be preoccupied with the "common man": Just as the Bible empowered the "common man" of Israel, the Homestead Act of 1863 enabled the "common man" in America to acquire assets and, thus, made people equal before the law. This, writes Berman (2008: 81), "underscored the philosophy that there is no equality without equity." There is no mention, of course, of all those indigenous populations that became disenfranchised and deprived of their rights in order to make "equity and equality" possible for whites.

A question we have to raise, if not answer, is why does Berman try to link the Bible with the founding fathers of American democracy? What drives his faulty and outrageous comparative project? He never tells us. Instead his third term, as is so customary in this apologetic literature, is missing or suppressed. It is left to us to guess. Perhaps it is to show that just as ancient Israel was unique among its polytheistic neighbors, the modern nation state of Israel is the same when compared to its undemocratic Arab neighbors? Since his audience is primarily American, perhaps his goal is to show that the United States and Israel share a biblical legacy and are unique unto themselves, which make them both singular among the nations?[9] It is certainly difficult to tell. What I do hope is obvious, however, is how Berman uses comparison to protect his own religion, unfortunately one of the hallmarks of the comparative method over the years.

The Introduction of Cognitive Science

In his *New Patterns for Comparative Religion* (2016), William E. Paden wants to take localized comparative endeavors and translate them onto the level of the human species. Moving from, in his own words, nouns to verbs, his interest is how groups "do" things. This includes activities such as transmitting mythic pasts and ritualizing life passages. So, while there might be "thousands of things humans and human groups do in common, and while many might seem obvious or trivial, they could still serve as points of comparison within the rich cultural examples that encompass them" (*ibid*.: 4). Paden, then, wants to move beyond the rich materiality and textuality that drives someone like Dempsey's analysis and instead examine religions from a cognitive or evolutionary model. Again, in his words:

> with our global, historical perspective, we in comparative religion are positioned to point out that patterns of religious behavior are themselves part of the subject matter when exploring how we have evolved as social beings. For instance what if, for our human species, transmitting accounts about the sacred foundations of one's world is itself a natural niche-building behavior for holding one's group together—and thus apiece with survival-fitness? (Paden 2016: 7)

For Paden, the comparative study of religion is a natural and desacralized activity. It ought to look for the general behind the particular. Unlike comparativists of an earlier generation, however, this general is not some amorphous notion of the sacred so much as it is evolutionary cognition and behavior. While he makes comparison, as well he should, into a mundane activity that refuses to privilege one form or expression over others, his next step is backwards, in my opinion, when he still wants to imagine something behind diverse cultural forms. Yet the pattern (what he calls "big concepts")

> need not suppress diversity and from an evolutionary perspective they are balanced out by the powerful role of diverse environments prompting diverse behaviors and versions of behaviors. So that does not reduce the human mind to sameness, or religion to a single trait, or override the role of cultural and gendered differences ... Quite the opposite: the evolutionary outlook tends to carve up or fractionate "religion" into its individual dispositions in settings where human actions are typically and variously generated from learned cultural skills and not just from simple default, uniform instinctual reactions. (Paden 2016: 230)

Paden tries to walk a very fine line, one that takes social activity seriously while simultaneously trying to be responsible to the cognitive science of religion. In so doing, however, he probably risks offending specialists in both fields. The attention to the specific means he only obtusely engages in research in the cognitive study of religion; and the attempt to get at the "big concepts" behind cultural specifics and his superficial engagement with actual religious traditions potentially alienates those interested in historical and textual study.

While I will take up some of the challenges posed by the cognitive science of religion in the final chapter, it suffices to mention in the present context that it also has the potential to reify human behaviors—only now imagined as part of some generic panhuman culture as opposed to the "sacred."

Conclusions

Comparison is something that, like beauty, exists solely in the eyes of the beholder. While the comparativist wants us to believe that the act s/he is undertaking is as natural as can be, it is not. Recall, for example, Prothero, whose entire comparative enterprise is predicated on the notions that religions run the world and motivate people to make certain choices over others. Or recall Dempsey, who wants us to imagine the sacred, even though she has no direct access to it, in the bodily and ritualistic actions of religious believers in different localized contexts.

In this chapter we have witnessed comparison take place at the micro level (Smith, Dempsey), the macro level (Prothero) and the theoretical level (Paden). However, none of these models, with the sole exception of Smith, affords us with a balance between theory and data. Successful comparison must involve immersion in languages, texts, traditions, *and* theory. One cannot compare unless one knows the languages *in their original*. One cannot compare, say, Arabic and Judeo-Arabic sources from the tenth century unless one actually can read these two languages. We have all seen the extremes to which grandiose comparative frameworks that pay precious little attention to actual sources can lead us. Here the work of Eliade might well be the most egregious example (other examples include Prothero 2010; Henderson 1991, 1998). Such examples provide little to no reflection on what it means to compare. It is simply done either to show the morphology of the sacred in the case of Eliade or similarities between reified entities in the case of the others.

Comparison is a theoretical activity, to be sure. Nevertheless, for it to be effective on a theoretical level, it must be able to account for the data. This means that we must be self-conscious and self-reflexive on the one hand, and possess all of the historical, literary, and textual skills on the other. We must thus speak to two discrete audiences: other comparativists, that is, scholars who work in different religious traditions but who deal with a similar problem; and non-comparativists who often work solely in one field. This is not an easy task. In fact, one might well say that it is impossible. How can one write for both specialists in history or area studies *and* scholars who work on religions other than one's own specialty? Whether or not we can actually do so, we must strive to accomplish this. If we do not then we risk either irrelevance or, even worse, charges of oversimplification.

Notes

1. This and the following section rework Hughes (2017).
2. The term *convivencia* was first used by Castro in his *The Spaniards* ([1948]1971). Although an invented term, it subsequently became part of Spanish academic vocabulary as attested by the term's perhaps uncoincidental inclusion in the 2001 dictionary produced by the Real Academia Española, which defines it simply as *acción de convivir* ("The act of living together"). In this regard see Junod (2012: 23).
3. Symbiosis, for example, is the basic rationale behind two recent reference works devoted to Jewish–Muslim relations—Stillman (2010) and Meddeb and Stora (2013). While I briefly examine the rationales here, I wish to make clear that I have no intention of either denigrating the tremendous contributions that both works make to our understanding of *specific* interactions, nor do I assume that all the contributors share the general vision of the editors. In his very short introduction to the massive and unprecedented five-volume *Encyclopedia of Jews in the Islamic World*, Stillman invokes the trope of "Judeo-Arabic symbiosis" in which

   > Jewish philosophy was created, and Jews took part in the economic and intellectual life of the medieval Islamic oikoumene on a scale unprecedented until the modern era. Hebrew language and literature underwent its most important revival prior to the Haskala (Jewish Enlightenment) and the emergence of Modern Hebrew as the only example of a revived vernacular. The Islamic Middle Ages also gave birth to the most important sectarian movement since Late Antiquity—Karaism which, despite its relatively small number of adherents had a profound impact as a catalyst upon majoritarian Rabbinic Judaism. (Stillman 2010: vii)

   In the introduction to their 1200-plus page *A History of Jewish-Muslim Relations: From the Origins to the Present Day*, Meddeb and Stora write of their goal: "the humble ambition of making contemporary research available to readers in order to propose a synthesis of the memories on both sides. It will serve as a preamble. The intention is that it will be continued, that it will prompt exchanges and dialogue" (Meddeb and Stora 2013: 16).
4. Michael Lecker has done the most work on the Jews of early Islam. However and unfortunately, he is largely uninterested in establishing

whether or not these Jews were normative or rabbinic and instead seems to assume that they were. See his comments in Lecker (1995: 21–28; 2005).

5. For a strong critique of Orsi's approach in the essay and his edited volume more generally, see Arvidsson (2013).
6. "Lived religion" (e.g., Tweed 1997; McGuire 2008) or "material religion" (e.g., Promey 2014; Plate 2015) seem to signal for their authors a new, more grounded emphasis in the study of religion, as if previous generations had somehow missed out on its actual "lived" or "material" aspects. But note that the term "religion" is never queried. It remains untouched and the emphasis is now on the adjective to describe it in more nuance than had previous generations of scholars.
7. The description may be found online at http://press.uchicago.edu/ucp/books/series/CLA200.html (the italics are mine).
8. This section reworks Hughes (2015b).
9. That the right-wing Tikvah Fund is behind this volume is another story (see Hughes 2013: 108–112).

Chapter 4

Contexts

If the old comparison was about the construction of grand narratives, the new comparison will, I hope, be about localized contexts. If the old way of doings things jettisoned the historical record in favor of the quest to find a timeless if ultimately unknowable essence that undergirds all religious forms and expressions, the new way will hopefully revel in the close and detailed study of the particular. No longer (and this is more a plea than a current reality) will comparison be used to show what it has always tended to show in the academic study of religion: either how two things are inherently different (and thus one of them is *sui generis*) or how they are essentially the same. If the former is about protecting one's own religion from foreign contamination, the latter holds out an ecumenical promise that, on a fundamental level, we are all ultimately the same, at least deep down inside. Yet, as I have tried to argue in previous chapters, these two traditional ends of the comparative continuum are less about scholarship than they are about apologetics. Juxtaposed against these two models, I have argued that comparison ought to function as a method that demonstrates how, to use a line from the biblical book of Ecclesiastes, there is nothing new under the sun. One's dataset functions as but one example that illumines a larger issue of human creativity. Comparison, then, is about choice. Not only do we choose what we think to be worthy of comparison, we also make the choice to show that what we study is illustrative of a broader issue or problem. Yet, surprisingly, many are rarely aware of either of these choices. We often think that what we compare is as natural as can be or that, while relevant to our own particular subfield, its significance is unable to transcend that subfield.

Even those who claim not to compare do so whether they know it or not or even whether they admit it or not. Comparison, appeals of those like Joseph Campbell to the contrary, is not the provenance of the generalist who desires to show how much one knows about *all* the religions of the globe. If anything, comparison should be about the exact opposite:

- to show that one knows one particular datum well;
- to show that one is interested in how scholars working with other data (including in other disciplines) but similar questions and problems deal with similar issues;
- to use their insights to illumine one's initial datum; and then
- to use one's own datum, in turn, to illumine that data and questions of others.

In previous pages, this means that our model for comparison should be something along the lines that Jonathan Z. Smith imagined as opposed to that of someone like Mircea Eliade.

If comparison has traditionally run roughshod over the mundane in the service of some amorphous transcendent meaning, comparison's future, I trust, will revel in the quotidian dimension of social facts. Comparison, in other words, ought not to be designed to make us better people by introducing us to the timeless and ageless wisdom of the world's religions. On the contrary, comparison ought, ideally, to show us how humans, as social actors, make meaning in their social worlds. The emphasis has to be on the making as opposed to the meaning since the latter is only constructed by means of the former. The focus, then, has to be on appreciating how religious meaning, like any meaning, is constructed without making appeals to divine causation or some essence—the so-called sacred—that various religious expressions are believed to manifest. Comparative religion, then, should not be interested in making a set of superficial comparisons between religions that one does not know particularly well; rather, it should demonstrate how certain questions generated by other scholars of religion, when framed properly, can illumine our own particular dataset and the questions we ask of it, in addition to showing how our data, when understood in a particular way, helps to expand further our understanding of these larger questions. Comparison, as I understand it, paradoxically emerges from a very specific body of literature and area of expertise.

Comparison, then, is about showing how our data exemplifies larger questions. In my own work on Judaism and Islam in the century or so after the death of Muhammad, for example, my primary interest is to show but one example of human ingenuity and creativity in the midst of social change and uncertainty. What, for example, do these social groups appeal to? How and for what purposes? Certainly this involves dealing with the relevant historical and linguistic traditions that often derive from their own highly specialized and often technical contexts. However, the point is that we have to remember that such contexts are not ends in and of themselves. It is finding this delicate equilibrium between technical work and general questions that ideally differentiates the job of the comparativist from that of those who work solely in specific areas or traditions.

Analysis between religions, or even within a religion, quite simply cannot take place on the level of ad hoc comparison. Such superficiality leads to frameworks—and the field of Religious Studies is littered with the remnants of these—where x is essentially the same as y (e.g., Jews have pilgrimages, Hindus have pilgrimages, ergo they both share a notion of pilgrimage that represents manifestations of some cross- or trans-cultural essence). This, not infrequently, returns us to the Eliadean hermeneutic of bringing to light the sacred's morphology. While many today would no doubt claim that such a hermeneutic was passé, they nonetheless continue to indulge in it albeit using different language. Comparison needs to be comprehensive, taking into consideration the interrelationships between a social worldview, a way of (social) life, and a view of the social order. It is this intersectionality that provides us with a nuanced picture of our data that, in turn, permits us to put it into counterpoint with other data with the understanding that our conclusions will show both similarities and differences, but definitely not a sameness that flattens everything.

Establishing Context

Whereas the previous chapter sought to show some of the possibilities that comparison can afford the student of religion, the goal of the present chapter is to explore some of the specific contexts in which to undertake comparison. When I write on a medieval Jewish philosopher, for example, it is only natural that I will look to immediate antecedents or contemporaries—ones that lived in the same environment and wrote in the same language or languages—to try to get a better sense of what that particular thinker was up to (e.g., Hughes 2004, 2007). This is because such an individual had read the work of these other individuals and, in the process, often comments and builds upon their ideas. The comparison thus has to be local. If they do not live within the same geographical orbit and speak (and write) the same language, the comparison falls apart. If they did not live in the same intellectual environment, while a comparison may be able to show certain similarities, it will only ever be circumstantial and based on happenstance.[1] This is why a comparison of, say, the Jew Abraham Ibn Ezra (1089–1167) with the Muslim Avicenna (980–1037) is productive because we possess material evidence that confirms that the former read the work of the latter and engaged with it. A similar comparison between Ibn Ezra and the Chinese thinker Confucius (551–479 BCE), however, is much more problematic since neither knew of the other's existence nor did they read the other's work.[2]

What, then, is a context? A context refers to the specific and localized circumstances that are responsible for the formation and setting of any event, locution, or idea. Understanding the context aids in analysis and description or, in the words of Geertz, is part and parcel of arriving at a so-called "thick description":

> it must be admitted that there are a number of characteristics of cultural interpretation which make the theoretical development of it more than usually difficult. The first is the need for theory to stay rather closer to the ground than tends to be the case in sciences more able to give themselves over to imaginative abstraction. Only short flights of ratiocination tend to be effective in anthropology; longer ones tend to drift off into logical dreams, academic bemusements with formal symmetry. (Geertz 1973: 24)

A thick description is one that explains not just a specific behavior, but that behavior's larger social context so that it becomes meaningful to others. It is not simply a description, but a redescription, that which translates an act or an utterance onto a scholarly and analytic register. Such a description, for Geertz and indeed for myself, is composed not only of facts but also of commentary on those facts, and subsequent interpretation and re-interpretations of those comments and original interpretations. The result, in an ideal world, will be an analysis that works on multiple levels: textual, social, economic, intellectual, ethnographic, and so on.

The comparativist has to pay attention to context, which means acknowledgment of that context's physical and communicative dimensions, which are simultaneously temporal, geographical, spatial, nominal, and semiotic. Manipulation of any of these dimensions results in a changed environment of interpretation. In so doing, to invoke Geertz again, our goal is "not to answer our deepest questions, but to make available to us answers that others ... have given, and thus to include them in the consultable record" of humanity (Geertz 1973: 30).

But note that by context I do not have in mind the notion, so prevalent in religious studies' circles, that we must take a practitioner's utterance or a believer's utterance at face value. Far from it. Indeed, if anything it is the idea that we must faithfully and accurately reproduce the beliefs of others that risks making religious studies into the laughing stock of the Academy. Scholarship in religion cannot simply be about outsiders or outside-insiders or inside-outsiders conveying the actions or beliefs of religious practitioners in their own words. A healthy dose of skepticism, criticism, in addition to the requisite need for redescription, is integral to all fields in both the humanities and the social sciences.

How Does One Locate a Context? Three Potential Models

Everything is a context because ultimately everything is contextual, the product of larger social, cultural, economic, and intellectual webs of meaning. Nothing exists in isolation. If something did it would be unknowable. The smaller the context the better: for example, a particular ritual or interconnected set of rituals, a text or interrelated set of texts, specific and localized historical interactions. This allows us to avoid examining religions (e.g., "Judaism" and "Islam") that, despite being one of the hallmarks of religious studies (in the sense that we teach courses on them, publish books on them, and so on), is actually a hindrance to analysis. Instead of focusing on disembodied religions writ large, attention needs to shift to specific interactions between groups that, staying with my example, either define themselves or are defined by others as Muslims and/or Jews.

In this section, I wish to examine three models that I find successful. I offer them not so much as models for emulation as to show how comparison can be effective when confined to local contexts. They all differ from one another, but what they share is an impressive knowledge of the relevant historical and literary/textual sources. Such a knowledge prevents each model from straying too far down the path of essentialism and, in the process, informs us that what we have been habituated to call religion is actually a much more mundane and complicated affair than phenomenology would have us believe. I also invoke these three models in order to put them in counterpoint with many of the rather poor attempts at comparison that I have documented over the previous chapters.

The first model comes by way of a comparison dealing with perhaps one of the most persistent and misused set of comparanda in religious studies, that between early Judaism and early Christianity.[3] These two traditions—recall Budde's model in Chapter 1—have been put in counterpoint for a host of apologetic reasons that are not infrequently designed to show the superiority of the latter at the expense of the former. In his *Border Lines* (2014), Daniel Boyarin seeks to examine this relationship in the late antique period, albeit with a new set of interpretive lenses. Comparison, for him, is not some vague or opaque set of similarities between two religions that is customarily put in a general narrative that runs something like the following: at some point in the second and/or third century, Christianity broke away from Judaism. Not unlike the narrative that creates and sustains the interrelationship between Judaism and Islam a few centuries later, one that I articulated in the previous chapter, such a narrative is more about apologetics than anything we might label as historical. In Christian theological circles this narrative usually takes the form of supersessionism with a spiritual Christianity transcending a more legalistic Judaism, one that often culminates in the claim that Christianity represents the true Judaism of the biblical prophets. In Jewish polemical sources, though not nearly as prevalent as the former, such polemics usually take the form of Judaism as the original form of monotheism, the *Urmonotheismus*, that gave birth to Christianity in the second century just as it would subsequently do to Islam in the seventh.

Moving beyond such simplistic and theologically inflected narratives, Boyarin seeks to nuance the model that imagines a clearly defined break of a single entity into two separate religions. Key here is that he does not take at face value all that later sources would have us believe, and that has provided the basic narrative for talking about the break between Judaism and Christianity for millennia, including the religious studies classroom. According to this model, there existed one religion, Judaism, which then took on a hybrid identity after the death of Jesus, namely those Jews who believed in Jesus and those who did not. But, and this is important for Boyarin's analysis, even before the division into Judaism and Christianity, there is often the assumption that there would have been certain beliefs and practices that would be identifiable as either Jewish or Christian. Boyarin seeks to challenge this thesis and instead argues, based on a close reading of the sources *in their original languages*, that no such characteristics that could neatly be identified as uniquely Jewish or uniquely Christian existed in the late antique period.

Rather, on Boyarin's reading, there existed groups of social actors, some of whom were Jesus-following Jews and some of whom were Jews who did not follow Jesus. All of these groups would have inhabited a shared social and intellectual space in which a wide variety of beliefs—such as a second divine being, Sabbath observance or keeping kosher—were widely distributed (Boyarin 2014: 13–16). The eventual creation and maintenance of border markers to separate these beliefs into "Judaism" and "Christianity" only occurred much later and were largely the product of "border markers"—heresiologists, theologians, among others—eager to construct discrete identities for their fellow practitioners. Such individuals were the ones responsible for moving groups, ideas, and behaviors to one side or another of what was then, but not later, an artificial border (*ibid.*: 15). In his own words:

> Once I am no longer prepared to think in terms of preexistent different entities—religions, if you will—that came (gradually or suddenly) to enact their difference in a "parting of the ways," I need to ask who it was in antiquity who desired to make such a difference, how did they accomplish (or seek to accomplish) that making, and what was it that drove them? ... My proposal here is that the discourse we know of as orthodoxy and heresy provides at least one crucial site for the excavation of a genealogy of Judaism and Christianity ... Authorities on both sides tried to establish a border, a line that, when crossed, meant that someone had definitely left one group for another. (Boyarin 2014: 2)

As Boyarin's work reminds us the "parting of the ways" between religions, caught up as it is in often later theological and apologetic agendas, is assumed rather than investigated. Yet, for some reason, we continue to accept and gullibly believe all that later ideological and often highly political works tell us—so much so that they become part of the scholarly narrative that supposedly defines their interrelationship to one another. This is because there has been a tendency in religious studies to misclassify such polemical and ideological works as religious or worse as "spiritual" texts. Traditional comparative approaches, for some reason, have preferred tidiness to messiness and simplicity to complexity. Since history is messy and complex, however, why do we persist with superficial comparison in the academic study of religion?

Whereas Boyarin is interested in how second and third century heresiologists engaged in a process of creating difference between Judaism and Christianity, his investigations are relevant to anyone working on the intersection of different social groups. For example, my own work on the "parting of the ways" between Judaism and Islam in the seventh and eighth centuries has drawn heavily on the theoretical apparatus that he and others who work on this material in a sophisticated manner have articulated. This is the perfect example of what I mentioned at the beginning of this chapter: my own particular datum of Jewish–Muslim social formation in the seventh and eighth centuries has much to learn from those scholars who work on a similar problematic but with different data. Our best model for understanding the formation of Judaism and Islam in the eighth century, I submit, is the model supplied by the formation of Judaism and Christianity several centuries earlier. This work provides both a technical and a theoretically rich vocabulary that is relevant to all those working on similar problems but in different temporal and geographic areas.

Perhaps significant is the fact that Boyarin was not trained in religious studies, nor does he work in the context of such a department. Instead, his training is in the technical field of rabbinics, a field that demands tremendous technical attention to Hebrew and Aramaic texts, including all of these languages' nuances. However, Boyarin, unlike many scholars of rabbinics, was not content to stay on the level of rabbinic texts, but instead has combined his knowledge of such texts with an attention to history and social theory. His interests in these last two areas facilitated his gravitation to the study of Christian origins, something that necessarily involves knowledge of Greek and other relevant languages. This is a far cry from the superficial treatment of linguistics and history that we witnessed in the work of those phenomenologists examined in previous chapters.

Boyarin's work shows the importance of context and the need to understand it. Since religions do not exist in the ether, but rather in specific social settings, it is incumbent upon the scholar of religion to be familiar with all of the relevant social, intellectual, cultural, and linguistic features of specific contexts, in addition to being attuned to critical theory. It is this combination—not one or the other, but both together—that enables the scholar of religion to do what he or she does and, in the process, facilitates the ability to speak coherently and cogently to colleagues who work with different datasets.

The second model I have in mind comes by way of Bruce Lincoln's *Theorizing Myth* (1999). Equal parts historical, linguistic, and political, the work seeks to show the reader how the category myth has been employed from antiquity to the present. *Mythos*, the Greek term from which our modern concept derives, he argues, was not simply a "likely story" that was different from the more rational *logos*. Instead, he shows how the victory of *logos* over *mythos* reflected struggles over political, linguistic, and epistemological authority occasioned by the expanded use of writing, including the eclipse of poetry by prose, and the consolidation of Athenian democracy. Myth, such a key word in the terminological toolkit of scholars of religion since at least the pioneering work of Friedrich Max Müller, becomes on Lincoln's cautious reading a tool that has been used to fetishize or deride certain kinds of stories, often those told by others. In his own words,

> It is a truism that there is much at stake in the words people use and how they happen to use them, just as there is much at stake in the stories they tell and how these stories get told. In the following pages, my chief goal is to tell a story about the stories others have told about the stories of others still, and my point is that one should treat all these narratives and metanarratives with considerable care and caution. (Lincoln 1999: ix)

If we could sum up Lincoln's hermeneutic it would be "cautious" and attentive to ideology that often hides within texts that are often presented as "religious." He is particularly attuned to how cultural practices provide insights into systems in which power and privilege are contested. Rather than study myths as manifestations of the sacred, he examines them as vehicles for ideology or, in his own words, "as ideology in narrative form" (*ibid*.: xii). In this regard, Lincoln turns his attention to the eighteenth and nineteenth centuries when myth became a privileged type of narrative, one located at the epicenter of Romanticism, nationalism, and the need for "likely" stories upon which to found modern nation-states. Lincoln's narrative seamlessly weaves together myths, scholarship on myths, and the ideology associated with fascism and nationalism to reveal how the actual mythic stories and the stories scholarship has told of those stories have allowed elites to encode their own privilege over others (*ibid*.: 153–155). These stories are not taxonomic, for which they are usually mistaken, but ideological.

Lincoln's narrative, then, is not about religion *per se*, but about the broader social, historical, and political processes that produce religious ideas. He refers to such religious discourses as sublimated human ones because they "use instruments that most often assist in the reproduction of the sociotaxonomic order to recalibrate that order by introducing new categories, eliminating old ones, or revising both categories and the hierarchic orders in which they are organized" (*ibid.*: 150). In the hands of Romantic thinkers, myth could now be used for a host of nationalist projects:

> This orientation takes for granted that nations, "cultures," and/or *Völker* (depending on the speaker's discourse) are primordial, bounded, unproblematic entities and that myth is the equally primordial voice, essence, and heritage of the group. Myth and group are understood to be linked in a symbiotic relation of co-reproduction, each one being simultaneously producer and product of the other. (Lincoln 1999: 210)

As with Boyarin, Lincoln works with limited contextual models that, by the end of his monograph, make a much larger point about scholarship, group identity, and the ways in which both become inscribed on the stories told. Like Boyarin, the force of Lincoln's comparison between stories and contexts derives from his knowledge of both the historical and linguistic materials that he studies. His footnotes, for example, reveal an impressive list of quotations and analysis from a host of Indo-European languages in their original.

Most importantly for me is that Lincoln attunes us to the fact that scholarship is not objective. On the contrary, scholarship has been and continues to be invested in a host of often non-scholarly interests. Within this context, just in case it needs repeating, comparison has rarely been about value-neutral juxtaposition, and more about other issues. These have run the gamut from the protective and the ecumenical to the nationalistic. It is incumbent upon us to uncover these dimensions in our work and the work of others to reveal what are the hidden assumptions of scholarship. Comparison, Lincoln shows us, has to involve a delicate balance between primary and secondary sources, between history and philology, and between texts and contexts.

The genealogy of terms and concepts is thus integral to the comparative method. Unless we understand where such terms and concepts come from, when they were initially deployed, by whom, and for what purposes, we risk making the same mistakes as our predecessors. In order to get where we are today, when we commonly frame questions in certain ways and widely share specific tools to pursue their answers, many intellectual and institutional battles were fought. Our questions and our tools, in other words, are not givens. On the contrary, as Lincoln's work so poignantly reminds us, they have been shaped by a host of intellectual and extra-intellectual activities. Lincoln reveals to us another site of comparison: how the terms and categories we employ with regularity to talk about religion have histories, often unsavory ones. Unless we understand these histories, and their wills to power, we risk making the very same mistakes as our predecessors.

My third model comes by way of Michael Sells's *Mystical Languages of Unsaying* (1994). Here, Sells examines the discourse of *apophasis* (i.e., "speaking away") that is a common feature of medieval mysticism. Apophasis seeks to reveal the impossibility of naming something that is ineffable by continually turning back upon its own propositions and names. It is thus a style of writing that mystics have historically employed in order to use language to get, paradoxically, beyond language (for a modern discussion of this topic, see Wolfson 2014). While Sells's comparative model is less context-based than the other two models I have presented in the sense that his analysis spans over 1000 years and is set in numerous geographical locales such as Avignon, Damascus, and Paris, his model nevertheless does this in such a way that representative texts from these diverse contexts speak to an overarching theme, namely, that of employing a particular textual strategy to speak about mystical experiences. But note that Sells is less interested in the contents of such experience—there is no mention, for example, of the sacred—than he is in the textual attempts to communicate such experiences.

Unlike Boyarin and Lincoln, Sells concerns himself with a set of textual strategies that seeks to create a new form of language that points to the aporia of transcendence (1994: 2). Again, it is worth mentioning that his goal is the study of textual forms that try to get at this silence and *not* to posit, à la phenomenologists of old, that it actually exists. This language of unsaying, in his words, forms

> the semantic analogue to the experience of mystical union. It does not describe or refer to mystical union but effects a semantic union that re-creates or imitates the mystical union ... Rather than pointing to an object, apophatic language attempts to evoke in the reader an event that is—in its movement beyond structure of self and other, subject and object—structurally analogous to the event of mystical union. (1994: 9–10)

In order to make the case for this, Sells examines several mystics held together by the Western tradition of apophasis: Plotinus (204–270), John the Scot Eriugena (815–877), Ibn Arabi (1165–1240), Marguerite of Porete (1250–1310), and Meister Eckhart (1260–1328). All of these individuals when read in their original languages and not through translations, he argues, sought to critique their own religious traditions while simultaneously trying to show what they considered the true meanings of their religions to be. Both of these features, Sells claims, manifested themselves in a particular way of writing that, though not confined to a particular historical context, nevertheless arise in particular contexts in particular individuals that, in their own ways and for their own purposes, are struggling with the ancient Greek notion of being and ontology.

The end result is that Sells shows us how mystical apophasis is "a cross-cultural mode of discourse, emerging out of a variety of religious and cultural traditions and sharing key semantic features" (1994: 201). Obviously while the doctrinal content of these diverse mystics (some Muslim, some Christian, and Plotinus who was neither) certainly differ from one another—in other words they are not all the same—there are certain similarities in the themes or tropes that run through them, such as "their respective use of apophatic language to speak of an eternal moment of mystical union that has always occurred and always is occurring" (ibid.: 206).

I have used a variation of this model in my own work into the genre of dialogue in Jewish philosophy (Hughes 2007), where I examined the use of dialogues in distinct Jewish cultures running from the eleventh to twentieth centuries. My goal, like Sells, was not to show that there existed some generic dialogue that manifests itself in these diverse cultures so much as it was to contextualize key dialogues and show what they had in common both with their immediate non-Jewish contexts *and* other Jewish dialogues from other temporal and geographical contexts. One can, in other words, look at specific contexts across temporal and geographical periods so long as one has some overarching question that links those contexts and periods together. Like Sells, I was not interested in positing a common religious or mystical experience, but to understand a similarly structured semantic event in different but related cultures.

A Case Study: Muslim and Jew in the Seventh Century

Allow me to give an extended example of a contextual comparison that shows, I trust, some of the issues that have arisen theoretically in this chapter.[4] This example, again, derives from my own research into the relationship between, for lack of a better term, "Jewish" and "Muslim" social groups in the first two centuries after the death of Muhammad in 632 CE. It is a period that is virtually obscure owing, among other things, to our paucity of data and this paucity is further confused by later sources attempting to pass themselves off as earlier ones. Even our default theorist of symbiosis, Shlomo Dov Goitein, had to admit that "the centuries both preceding and following the rise of Islam are the most obscure in Jewish history" (Goitein 1955: 95), thereby shattering his earlier confidence in the normativity of Arabian Judaism. This aporia, however, did not stop him nor has it stopped other modern commentators from projecting later ideas onto the period in question (e.g., Newby 1988; Mazuz 2014). More often than not this has involved positing a normative rabbinic Judaism, defined by what was going on in the later court of Baghdad, and then assuming that it somehow existed at the time of Muhammad and in such a manner that it was either removed from or developed untouched by its immediate Arabo-Islamic environment. A further assumption in much of this literature is that Islam simply appears doctrinally and liturgically fully formed at the time of Muhammad. Overlooked in all of these narratives are all the theoretical and sectarian debates that took centuries to work out and that were ultimately responsible for what would become normative Sunni and normative Shiite teaching.

Despite the fact that well over three-quarters of world Jewry lived within Islamic lands until the tenth century, we cannot hide the fact that our understanding of Jews during the late antique period is minimal at best or non-existent at worst. Perhaps the one thing that it is possible to say with at least a modicum of confidence is that Judaism, not unlike Islam, was poorly defined at this particular time and in this particular locale. It was a time of political and social uncertainty witnessed, for example, by the power vacuum caused by the fall of the Byzantine and Sasanian Empires, a feature that was directly responsible for the concomitant rise of groups engaged in messianic and apocalyptic speculation. Many of these groups—later written off as "heterodox"— explored different paradigms of leadership and structures of authority (Grossman 1984: 15-44; Wasserstrom 1988), and many of them shared a similar semantic and apocalyptic worldview no doubt the result of the chaotic political situation. Contrary to the symbiotic model that has a normative rabbinic Judaism helping to create a normative Islam, it is impossible to sort through normative and non-normative groups, let alone to decide who took what from whom or when. We should also not overlook the fact that, though later sources would write many of these groups off as "heterodox," they were anything but at the time since orthodoxy had yet to be established. It was an environment, in other words, wherein doctrinally ill-defined social groups—some of which would later become Shiite, Sunni, or rabbinic groups—interacted freely with one another and would have been recognizable to each other.

On the "Jewish" side of things, paradoxically we primarily know of the existence of many of these groups from Muslim sources, such leadership paradigms ranged from the highly messianic and apocalyptic to what would eventually become normative. The key, though, is that we not assume an early normativity from which departed a number of heterodox groups. Only after the fact would they be written off as heterodox. In the complex social situation that enshrouded Judaism at this period and in this region we learn the names of many individuals, groups, and institutions, but since the rabbis eventually carried the day and often gave their ideological enemies the silent treatment (Feldman 1993: 35-38), we know very little about them. It is also important to realize that while rabbinic Judaism was emerging as the regnant form of Judaism in Baghdad and environs in this period, this did not necessarily mean that it was regnant for all Jews throughout the burgeoning Islamic empire, especially in places like the easternmost regions of Persia, a place that witnessed the rise of numerous messianic movements, and was, among other things, the home of a number of highly messianic proto-Shiite groups known as the *ghulat*. On these margins of empire, I wish to argue, we witness an overlap between numerous Jewish and Muslim social groups responding, often in the same way, to the social, religious, and intellectual turmoil brought about by the rapid spread of Islam and the concomitant process of Islamicization.[5] Such an overlap, in addition to paying close attention to historical detail, will hopefully show just how ridiculous a comparative model that wants to imagine a monolithic Judaism and a monolithic Islam interacting at this period is.

While Muhammad's message would certainly have drawn on some of the messianic and apocalyptic themes of late antiquity (Howard-Johnston 2011; Bowersock 2012; Stroumsa 2015a: 59–100), tropes of borrowing or influencing are impossible to ascertain. Jewish–Muslim groups, Jewish–Christian groups, Christian–Muslim groups, and so on would have existed in an environment in which ideas were shared as opposed to being seen as part of one half of these dyadic terms.[6] Indeed, we should also note that the hyphen in all of these groups may well artificially separate what in fact was not separated or separable. Perhaps it is better to talk, for example, of Jewmuslims or Muslimjews, realizing that our inherited vocabulary may not do the situation on the ground justice. Muhammad's apocalyptic message certainly would have appealed to *some* of these groups, some of which would certainly be enfolded into his nascent polity. However, to return to our narrative of symbiosis: this is not tantamount to Judaism functioning as a midwife to Islam. If anything what we have is doctrinally underdefined social groups slowly giving definition to what would become Sunnism, Shiism, and rabbinic Judaism at the center, with that center eventually writing these groups off as heterodox.

One such group is the Isawiyya. This group's emergence corresponds to the fall of the Umayyad caliphate in 750 (i.e, roughly a century after Muhammad's death), the rise of the Abbasid one, and the existence of a plethora of loosely connected and largely underdefined proto-Shiite *ghulat* ("extremist") groups (most recently, see Asatryan 2016). Shlomo Pines (1966: 237–249), for example, has argued that Abu Isa al-Isfahani (late seventh/early eighth century), the leader of this (for lack of a better term) Jewish sect, was probably influenced by a combination of Jewish and Christian beliefs similar to that found in other contemporaneous apocalyptic texts such as the *Doctrina Iacobi*, a seventh-century Greek Christian text that records the existence of a prophet in Arabia at the time of the birth of Islam.[7] Again, a narrative framework that works with a discrete Judaism, Islam, and Christianity fails to do this material justice. My brief analysis here relies on the important discussion of Wasserstrom, who has done more than anyone else to show the filiations between the Isawiyya and sectarian Muslim groups. For example:

> The early Muslims did not borrow their Messiah from Judaism, nor was Jewish Messianic imagery lent by a Jew to a Muslim in the sense that a lender lends to a debtor. Rather, Muslims consciously and creatively reimagined the Messiah. These Islamic rereadings, consonant with the decentralized pluralism of the Jewish redeemer myths, never pronounced one image of the Messiah as definitive. There were, of course, no councils of Judaism or Islam to rule on the officially proper Messiah. (Wasserstrom 1995: 57)

With no monolithically Jewish sense of what or who a Messiah was or should be, such groups could rely upon a prophetic vocabulary supplied by Muslim sectarian groups (some of which would eventually go on to be labeled as "Shiite"), just as Muslim groups recycled Jewish motifs without necessarily knowing their origins. These groups, of course, were not historians nor were they interested either in ascertaining who had what first or what was authentically "Jewish" or "Muslim"—both of these being the conceits of later heresiologists and modern scholars of religion. What we do know, however, is that Abu Isa's quasi-political, quasi-religious sectarian creation, the Isawiyya, remained one of the most important sectarian movements in Judaism, along with the Karaites, until the seventeenth century. According to the Muslim heresiographer al-Shahrastani (1086–1153), writing considerably after the fact, Abu Isa claimed that

> He was a prophet [*nabi*] and a prophetic messenger [*rasul*] of the awaited Messiah [*al-masih al-muntazar*]; that the Messiah has five harbingers [*rusul*] who precede him one after the other...than the Messiah is the best of the children of Adam; that he is of a higher status that the foregoing prophets [*anbiya*]; and that since he is his own apostle, he is the most excellent of them. He enjoined faith in the Messiah, exalting the mission [*da'wa*] of the harbinger; he believed that the harbinger is also the Messiah. (Wasserstrom 1995: 68)

It is worth noting that many of the Arabic terms in this paragraph would have been recognizable to many proto-Shiite groups, who used them in their own attempts to make sense of their social worlds. Abu

Isa thus combines "Jewish" and "Muslim" messianic vocabularies—or, perhaps better a "Jewmuslim" or "Muslimjewish" messianic vocabulary—in such a manner that he is comprehensible to both groups. Rather than say that one "influences" the other, it might be more apposite to imagine them as intimately linked, with full separation and claims of provenance only occurring much later. Again, according to Wasserstrom, the Isawiyya

> could be recognized as Jews by (Rabbanite and Karaite) Jews because they seemed Judaically orthoprax, and could be recognized as believers (by Kharijite and Shiite) Muslims because they seemed Islamically orthodox. This was, perhaps, an unwieldy if not spurious symmetry. (Wasserstrom 1995: 79)

It is this paradox, the lack of clarity between Jew and Muslim, which makes groups such as the Isawiyya so interesting. Such groups beard the likes of Eliade and many others discussed in this volume in their den by showing us clearly that the historical record is not a record of monolithic and disembodied religions interacting with one another and doing so, moreover, in ways that are devoid of social, intellectual, economic, and other non-"religious" concerns. Both Muslim and Jew, neither Muslim nor Jew, social groups like the Isawiyya occupy the margins of history. But, and this is key, they paradoxically are the ones responsible for giving definition to the center while at the same time subject to further marginalization. So while the Isawiyya will rarely appear in so-called normative histories of Judaism or in classes on Jewish history, at the time they provided a valid socioreligous framework that only in retrospect became labeled as heterodox.

Doctrinally, Abu Isa claimed, or at the very least his followers claimed him, to be the last of the five heralds from God who were responsible for announcing the arrival of the Messiah and the end of days (see Pines 1966; Wasserstrom 1995: 84–88; Stroumsa 2015a: 76–77). He acknowledged Jesus and Muhammad as true prophets, but only to their own followers—and here he seems to have been part of the same social environment that produced works such as *Doctrina Iacobi* and the *Secrets of Rabbi Shimon bar Yohai*, to be discussed presently. Abu Isa interestingly was not an antinomian and believed in some notion of Jewish law (*halakhah*) and observance of the holy days, which permitted his followers to "intermarry" with normative rabbinic Jews.

After his messianic claims, Abu Isa led some sort of messianic uprising before perishing in battle. This, however, was not the end of the Isawiyya. Indeed, according to Wasserstrom, the Isawiyya existed as a discrete Jewish sect for at least another three centuries (ibid.: 89). They were not, as some later scholars of Jewish-Muslim relations want to make out, a short-lived or anomalous messianic movement (see Cohen 1974: 416–422). Indeed, they show up frequently in subsequent Muslim literature, especially heresiologies, where they often receive a larger treatment than more normative rabbinic groups. Maimonides, writing in the twelfth century, could still write of Abu Isa and the Isawiyya that there

> was an exodus of a multitude of Jews, numbering hundreds of thousands from the East beyond Isfahan, led by an individual who pretended to be the Messiah. They were accoutered with military equipment and drawn swords, and slew all those that encountered them. According to the information I have received, they reached the vicinity of Baghdad. This happened at the beginning of the reign of the Umayyads. (Maimonides 1985: 127)

Despite the fact the he mentions the revolt, Maimonides, true to rabbinic practice, refuses to provide us with the name of Abu Isa. Although Maimonides puts the date of the uprising earlier than al-Shahrastani does, the messianic forces—on Maimonides's reading—are stopped by the caliph on the outskirts of Baghdad with a group of (normative?) Jewish sages, who ask the leaders of rebellion who their instigator was. They replied, "This man here, one of the descendants of David, whom we know to be pious and virtuous. This man whom we knew to be a leper at night, arose the following morning healthy and sound" (ibid.: 128). The sages subsequently inform Abu Isa's followers that they are incorrect in their interpretation and that, to them, he possesses none of the marks of the Messiah. The caliph then made them return home and "ordered them to make a special mark on their garments, the writing of the word cursed, and to attach one iron bar in the back and one in the front" (ibid.).

Maimonides's retelling of the story neatly encapsulates the tensions between centers and margins in the Jewish world under early

Islam. It is a rebellion, too, that neatly foreshadows the Abbasid revolution—an armed and messianic rebellion based on still inchoate Shiite doctrine then developing in the Eastern provinces of the burgeoning Empire (see Sharon 1983: 17-28; Arjomand 1994) and that subsequently marched on Damascus.

We get yet another glimpse of this Jewish-Islamic milieu in the apocalyptic *Secrets of Rabbi Shimon bar Yohai*, also composed in the mid-eighth century, also apparently associated with a Persian (= marginal) context.[8] This work, written at the end of the Umayyad caliphate and at the beginning of the Abbasid one—namely, a time of rapid political and social change that gave rise to messianic and apocalyptic speculation—identifies Muhammad as the fulfillment of Jewish messianic speculation. Here we have, then, an ostensibly "Jewish" text that resembles on many levels an "Islamic" one and that uses the same symbolism, vocabulary, and imagery—once again making a mockery of models like symbiosis. The work ends with the hope for the restoration of the Temple in Jerusalem that will be associated with the beginnings of the Abbasid revolution, both of which will usher in an apocalyptic battle between Israel and Byzantium, followed by the Final Judgment. Jewish messianic groups here have tied their lot to Muslim messianic groups. Near the beginning of the text, Metatron—an individual who figures highly in both Jewish and Islamic angelology (see Wasserstrom 1995: 181-205)—informs Rabbi Shimon that

> because of their oppression of Israel, the Holy One, blessed be He, sends Ishmaelites against them, who make war against them in order to save Israel from their hands. Then a crazy man possessed by a spirit arises and speaks lies about the Holy One, blessed be He, and he conquers the land, and there is enmity between them and the sons of Esau. (Lewis 1950: 313)

The Secrets of Rabbi Shimon bar Yohai is remarkable in the sense that an ostensibly "Jewish" document recycles Muslim apocalyptic speculation, some of which had already been paradoxically recycled from Jewish sources by early Muslims. Again, rather than imagine this as borrowing or influence, we should see it as collective worldmaking in an environment wherein ideas moved freely between porous boundaries. The result is that it is impossible to know with any degree of precision what is "Jewish" and what is "Muslim."

The eastern reaches of the growing Islamic empire were a hotbed of messianic fervor and apocalyptic speculation, and in participating in this environment, Jews and Muslims, on the margins, did not differ from one another. Indeed, if anything they seem to have been indistinguishable since they both saw the other as invested in the same apocalyptic drama that focused on Jerusalem and the coming End of Days. We see this clearly in texts like the *Secrets of Rabbi Shimon bar Yohai*, which shares a vocabulary of political uncertainty, messianic revolution, and armed revolt. Again, though, this was less a conscious borrowing in the sense that no one cared or even knew who had what first. It was the case of a well-worn stock of themes, vocabularies, and motifs crossing porous boundaries. Islam, or at least *certain* social groups making appeals to *certain* messianic impulses in what would subsequently emerge as Islam, become responsible for the messianic redemption of Jews in the Holy Land, at least according to *certain* Jewish social groups (Shoemaker 2011: 248–258).

I have used this extended example as a concrete way to show how I conceive of the task of comparison. As I have argued throughout this chapter, effective and informed comparison must move beyond simplistic characterizations that see monolithic religions interacting with one another. Religions, to reiterate, do not interact, but individuals and social groups do. This is why comparison has to proceed cautiously and on the level of smaller and more intimate contexts than disembodied and capital-R religions so that we can witness specific encounters that enable us, invoking Geertz again, to describe and understand "thickly." Comparison, as I trust this example has shown, has to be grounded in the historical record, sensitive to the textual tradition, and, at the same time, be theoretically sophisticated.

Gone, though we should certainly not forget lest we reproduce, are the times when we speak about how a reified and monolithic "Judaism" bumps up against a reified and monolithic "Islam." This narrative, and all that follows in its wake, is quite simply not helpful and produces a set of superficial comparisons, for my example, that did not even exist yet. Juxtaposed against such a model, I here tried to taxonomize and analyze specific and localized interactions between messianic groups who either identified as or were identified by others as somehow "Jewish" (e.g., the Isawiyya) with those who identified as or were identified by others as "Muslim" (e.g., *ghulat*) in the context of early eighth-century Iran. These social groups, certainly undefined or underdefined compared to later centuries, shared a common messianic vocabulary that took shape in response to the political instability associated with the rapid expansion of a still inchoate Islam.

Understanding such groups, I submit, reveals a number of key items. First, we see how identity, not to be confused with the models imagined from later centuries, is very fluid. So much so that it is impossible to say with any degree of certainty who is whom and/or who had what first. This completely undermines the symbiotic model that has tended to be our default model since at least the late nineteenth century. Second, this example has shown that comparison is not about finding timeless and eternal meanings in the world's religions. On the contrary, comparison ought to be a very mundane activity that treats social actors and not theological locutions. These social actors are not trying to find religious meaning, but are attempting to make sense of their very chaotic social worlds. In this they are not unlike other social groups in other geographical and temporal contexts. They are not the same as them, however, and this is why groups like the Isawiyya function as but one—one of many—examples of human creativity in the face of rapid social change. Third, without knowledge of the linguistic, social, and historical contexts it is impossible to engage in any sort of meaningful comparison. The traditional phenomenological model, while trying to make us feel good by positing that all religions represent but manifestations of the sacred, ought rather to make us uncomfortable. In positing sameness, phenomenology paradoxically dismisses human creativity and thereby deprives social actors of both their humanity and their autonomy.

Conclusions

This chapter has sought to offer insight into how comparison ought to work. It did this by arguing that, unlike the grand comparative schemas of the past, we ought to remove traditional and unhelpful slogans—like "religion," "Judaism," "Islam," and so forth—and instead pay attention to mundane and quotidian concerns as social actors, in specific times, places, and spaces, make sense of themselves and their social worlds. Rather than claim that "Judaism says x" or that "according to Muslims, y is the case," we need to focus on what particular individuals and groups do. There is no other way to do this other than by reading the texts that such groups produced and by understanding the historical contexts in which they lived. These texts, especially non-normative ones, are not representative of an entire religious tradition, but of particular groups who may either identify or be identified as part of that larger tradition.

Comparison, in sum, is about attention to contexts. Without such attention, we return to the morphological structure of classic phenomenology. In this respect, the historical record offers one of the most potent antidotes to the superficial analyses that phenomenology provides.

Notes

1. This is not to say that the comparison will yield interesting insights. In this regard, see Sells (1994), to be discussed in greater detail below.
2. Though this has not stopped some from trying to engage in such comparison. In this regard, see, for example, Lobel (2011: 82–97). Though I should note that although her position is in religious studies, she is not particularly interested (nor should she necessarily have to be) interested in the theory behind comparison. She, like many others in our field, just "does" it.
3. For a history of this nefarious use of comparison in dealing with Christian origins, consult Smith (1990).
4. Parts of this section rework Hughes (2017).
5. More generally, see Cameron (2012: 168–190); also al-Azmeh (2014: 1–46).
6. Though, as Stroumsa (1985) has duly noted, we must also not forget the messianism associated with Manichaean texts, which also date to this period. This, of course, adds another layer to the puzzle and further attests to the need to avoid easy typologies.
7. On the Jewish–Christian context of early Islam, see more recently Crone (2016), Stroumsa (2015b), Zellentin (2013: 150–153), and El-Badawi (2013: 138).
8. On the work, see Steinschneider (1874) and Shoemaker (2011: 28–31). An English translation may be found in Lewis (1950); and on the place of Jerusalem more generally, see Ofer Livne-Kafri (2001, 2006).

Chapter 5

Future

In this final chapter I would like to address what, if any, future the comparative enterprise might or should have in the academic study of religion. There are, of course, several possible futures open to this method, and certainly some are more rigorous than others. If previous chapters have surveyed the genealogy of the term, some of the uses to which the method has been put, and the epistemological and spiritual excesses it produces when unaccompanied by self-criticism and the requisite self-reflexivity (e.g., why this and not that?), the present chapter seeks to chart a way forward. This path, however, will not necessarily be an easy one as there still exist many who desire to use comparison for a host of non- or extra-academic purposes.

A cautiously and narrowly defined comparison, of the type that I offered at the end of the previous chapter, can and indeed must be rehabilitated in the academic study of religion, if in fact it ever existed. In that context, comparison successfully undermined traditional and regnant models of group interaction and, in the process, aided in our efforts to rethink traditional understandings of identity. This, however, does not necessarily mean that many will not want to return to the surfeit witnessed in the past. Comparison, after all, has always been more about privilege and denial than anything else, and there is no reason to doubt that it will still continue to be used for such purposes. The key, though, is to ensure that such frameworks in religious studies are called out for what they are. In these remaining pages, I want to examine some of the possible futures of comparison in the field by providing brief surveys of some recent studies that themselves seek to rein in comparison's excesses.

© Equinox Publishing Ltd. 2017

A quick perusal of many of these models, however, does not necessitate confidence. The grand old narratives of yesteryear unfortunately still predominate, and such narratives do not appear to be going anywhere in the near future. Those creating them today now tend to work in the cognitive science of religion (CSR) and many tend to labor under the assumption that they, too, are scientific in their inquiries. Here it might be worthwhile recalling the statement of Frank Byron Jevons, whom we encountered in Chapter 1. For him, "to make this use of the science of religion, we must fully and frankly accept the facts it furnishes" (Jevons 1908: ix). These furnished "facts," it will be recalled, were the truth claims of one particular religion, to wit, the author's own, and the goal of the comparative enterprise was "to convert men to Christianity" (*ibid.*).[1] Science and the objectivity afforded by its shadow would still seem to predominate—though now filtered through other channels.

While today such overly prejudicial statements as uttered by Jevons are thankfully very rare in the academic study of religion, we cannot overlook the fact that its nemesis, that which stresses similarity and sameness, is still regnant. The phenomenological model, with its continued talk of the sacred, its attempts to uncover its morphology, still imagines all of the religions of the globe as different paths to the same goal. In this, little has changed today from the excesses witnessed in the 1960s. While phenomenology has now morphed into neo-phenomenology, an approach (I do not want to call it a method) that, while aware of these past excesses, nevertheless still continues to talk about the sacred and the importance of an ecumenical or interfaith framework. Indeed, I think it is fair to say that neo-phenomenology, whether or not it goes by this name is irrelevant, is not a method in the academic study of religion but remains *the* method par excellence, and continues to represent the status quo. However, it is not methodical at all—it continues to be based on the idiosyncratic whims of the interpreter and is used haphazardly. Neo-phenomenology, likes its genealogical predecessor, continues to obscure difference as it simultaneously arranges "facts" to fit often predetermined conclusions. While it may be somewhat less hesitant to speak of monolithic religions, it is still interested in talking about the sacred, thereby engaged, Sisyphus-like, in the practices of isolating and describing that which can be neither isolated nor described. While it may make us feel good to show that all religions, and thus all people, are ultimately engaged in similar quests for the same meaning, scholarship is not necessarily meant to make us feel better about the spiritual health of our neighbors and the world which we inhabit.

The "Keep on Keepin' On" Model

We must not overlook the fact, then, that one very major possibility for the future of comparison is its past, and the continuation of its present. The definition and use of comparison, tuned now in what I have called a neo-phenomenological key, for a host of ecumenical reasons is still alive and well, and does not appear to be going away anytime soon. Witness, for example, Jeffrey J. Kripal's comments in his recent textbook titled *Comparing Religions*: "I have come to conclude that actual historical human encounters with the sacred *are* uncanny, *are* fantastic, indeed they are often so strange that we cannot possible exaggerate this weirddom" (Kripal 2014: xiii; his italics). The sacred is just assumed to exist, and, once again, the goal of the academic enterprise of religious studies is reduced to studying human interactions with it. The sacred, according to this hermeneutic, is neither constructed nor imagined, neither patrolled nor used for ideological ends, it just is and its existence is simply taken for granted. Kripal's comments come from his textbook that fancies itself as "a next-generation textbook which expertly guides, inspires, and challenges" his students and other readers. Yet, in the same sentence he informs us, using language that we have encountered time and again in the previous pages: students have to "think seriously" about religion in order to appreciate "religious pluralism in the modern world." Words in this description—taking religion "seriously" and "religious pluralism"—should alert us that very little has changed. Kripal, despite his own claims to the contrary, still seeks to understand humanity's "encounter with the sacred," which is described as being beyond reason or, in his own words, as simply "weird."

Or, consider a comparative book that won the American Academy of Religion's 2015 Award for Excellence in the Study of Religion for constructive-reflective studies. In her *Tastes of the Divine: Hindu and Christian Theologies of Emotion* (2014), Michelle Voss Roberts entertains the question of how the study of beliefs and practices in one tradition can illumine those of another. Using her ethnographic study of Indian and South Asian Hindu rituals, Roberts seeks to "bring new theological space to explore Christian practice" (*ibid.*: 5). Hindu ritual is thus meant to inform Christian ritual on the level of religious experience, what she had earlier referred to as "goose-bump moments" (*ibid.*: xv). These moments, for her, revolve around three "sentiments": "the transcendence of a soul at peace, the passion of a heart in love, and the liberating energy of fury at injustice" (*ibid.*: xvi). The job of comparison, at least on her reckoning, would seem to be based on the personal fancy or experience of the author. Again, like the phenomenology of old, the idiosyncratic is elevated to a hermeneutic or methodology. She continues,

> The beauty and wisdom of Hindu traditions excite me for many of the same reasons as the monumental works of Western classical music. The peace of meditation resonates with the bliss of absorption in a great work of art. The intimacy of devotional love in the *bhakti* traditions touches some of the same affects and desires. And whenever I find myself deep in conversation with learned Hindus, I find myself asking the same urgent ethical question: What do inner peace and love for the divine have to do with peace in our world and love of the other? (Roberts 2014: xvii)

Comparison, for Roberts as for many in the guild of religious studies, is about experience and, ultimately, about making the world a better place. While noble, such desires, I would argue, have little role in the comparative enterprise. If we are looking to understand our experiences and those of others and, in the process, improve Christian worship and transform souls, we risk overlooking all those beliefs and practices that do not conform to such desires. What about the political, the violent, and the unsavory? Too often these latter are written off as irrelevant to the sacred, or as features that risk impugning its inner or spiritual pureness. As a scholarly method, however, this produces tunnel vision, something that is certainly not an academic virtue. Scholarship must be an intellectual activity, not a spiritual one:

its goal is to understand the social worlds of others and, in the process, if we so desire (and there is no reason why we must do this), illumine something of the makeup of our own social worlds. Comparison shows us that all humans make meaning for themselves. The meaning is a corollary of the making and not vice versa.

As if to show us that nothing is ever new in the academic study of religion, Roberts invokes in the above quotation the term "bliss," a word that played such a monumental role in the comparative framework of Joseph Campbell ("follow your bliss"), with which I began this study. "Bliss," at least according to its dictionary definition, is "complete happiness." It is, in other words, like so much of the jargon associated with neo-phenomenology, an inner and subjective state, one that is impossible to verify or measure by any external or objective criteria. But this is precisely the point of Roberts' study: experience is personal and subjective, and thus not subject to political or cultural manipulation. Using the Indian framework of "rasa," loosely defined as emotion or taste, Roberts then suggests that Christian scholars, theologians, and practitioners can reexamine and experience the Divine—whatever this may be, she never tells us, or at least never tells us using the analytical language of customary scholarly practice—in their own tradition through the moods and affects that she witnesses in Hinduism. Comparative theologians, according to her,

> do not feign objectivity but acknowledge their starting point within particular religious traditions. They endeavor to understand another religious tradition by reading texts, often under the tutelage of practitioners or commentaries, and often in original languages. The comparative moment happens when they consider these sources of wisdom—which might also include practices, rituals, or aesthetic objects—alongside those of their home traditions. The categories and questions of the other tradition provide new lenses for viewing materials that were once familiar. (Roberts 2014: xx)

Although the preceding pages did not explicitly engage the subject of comparative theology (for a further example see Clooney 2005), preferring instead to lump this term under the rubric of phenomenology and then of so-called neo-phenomenology, Roberts now forces us to confront it head-on. As we see here, comparative theology does not start with an intellectual problem, but a spiritual one. One's "home tradition," largely familiar, is in need of some sort of rehabilitation or renaissance, which the study of other religions' "sources of wisdom" can provide. One learns about these sources of wisdom, on Roberts reading, though the "tutelage" of authentic "practitioners and commentaries." These gurus presumably provide the requisite insights to recognize anew the "sacred" in the home tradition. But these gurus are always the normative ones and voices from the margins are rarely, if ever, entertained.

That Roberts's monograph received an award of excellence from the American Academy of Religion is also surely worthy of note. It is reflective of how that Academy, the largest of its kind devoted to the study of religion, views comparison at the present moment. This view, I would suggest, has not changed dramatically since the heyday of Eliade's phenomenology. This approach, then, is very much one possible future of what the future of comparison might look like: it just keeps on keepin' on.

The Area Studies Model

Then again, another possible future is one wherein comparison is seen as outmoded, the product of a bygone era, and something that should be relegated to the field's dark basement. In this dystopian future, religious studies risks becoming so balkanized that it becomes little more than an administrative canopy under which awkwardly cohabit a set of relevant area studies—Buddhist studies, Jewish studies, Hindu studies, Islamic studies, and so on. Largely unrecognizable to one another, all that unites them is the administrative unit or some sort of empty slogan that is believed to enfold them. I would submit that many departments of religious studies, rhetoric to the contrary aside, are akin to this model. While some might relish the thought of religious studies reverting to the areas and the traditional interpretation of data (textual, critical editions, avoidance of large questions), this possible future would mean that there are nothing but areas— no questions or concerns that connect research in diverse topics and geographical contexts. Comparison may well take place within these areas—e.g., a set of Muslim texts from the tenth century—but interest in how these texts contribute to larger human meaning is largely forfeited in the service of localized concerns.

This is a tricky matter, however. As I argued in the previous chapter, comparison must be attuned to specific contexts. This means one must possess the requisite and often highly technical knowledge of a broad set of historical, linguistic, textual, and other social skills that permit one to analyze meaningfully the data in question. One must, in other words, be able to speak and be comprehensible to those in area studies. If one cannot, one risks resembling a Joseph Campbell or a Mircea Eliade from generations past. Yet, as I also suggested, this highly technical skill set should occupy about only three-quarters of the comparativist's conceptual tool box. The other quarter, if indeed we even want to quantify their percentages, has to consist in:

1. an explicit acknowledgment that one's data are not unique and thus are relevant to a larger audience than just those in one's own specialized area;

2. a desire to look to how this topic has been treated and is treated by other scholars using different data;

3. more than a passing familiarity with critical theory (both in the study of religion and cognate fields); and

4. the imagination to translate one's own data and/or set of questions to a larger setting.

All our collective subfields are ripe with these types of technical analysis. In rabbinics not infrequently we read studies that are so specific as to be completely out of bounds for the non-specialist or even the scholar of Judaism working in other areas.[2] Even though such works are ostensibly written by scholars of religion, with PhDs in religious studies, and who work within departments of religious studies, they work completely in their own niches with little or no regard for larger comparative issues. The other side of this is those scholars, especially many within the subfield of Islam, that are so interested in portraying Islam in a positive light by stressing what is (or is not) an authentic representation that they have largely ceased to be critical scholars, but liberal theologians (my critique of this approach may be found in Hughes 2015a). Caught up in identity politics and post-colonial critiques that emphasize victimhood, many of these studies are engaged in little more than special pleading.

So while comparison can only emerge from specific areas, it paradoxically has to transcend its specificity. Comparison, to reiterate the general theme of this volume, is about finding an equilibrium between field and subfield, texts and contexts, area studies and disciplinarity. Without this delicate balance we witness either superficiality on the one hand or insularity on the other.

Cognitive Science of Religion and Comparison

Another possible future for the comparative enterprise is one that removes pretty much all historical context and instead defers comparison to the level of species. Within this approach, the specificity of distinct cultures recedes into the background at the expense of locating some panhuman type of behavior. Previous archetypes of meaning that emphasize essences or the sacred have here transformed into archetypes of human cognition. In his *New Patterns for Comparative Religion* (2016), which I examined earlier, William E. Paden argues as follows:

> While the notion of a "psychic unity of mankind" became an object of postmodern derision, the newer cognitive/evolutionary approaches to religion are a distinct move to recapture the psychic unity or commonality at a species level underlying the surface of cultural differences. At the level of culture, comparability of meanings flounders; it is the nature of culture and cultural location to be environmentally different with regard to systems of signification. But at the evolutionary level of human behavior, comparability abounds. (Paden 2016: 174)

Paden here maintains that, while specific cultural contents might be important, underlying them is a specific genetic disposition that is common to the entire species. One searches in vain, however, for Paden to actually employ this in a concrete example of comparison, such as that which I did at the end of the previous chapter. Instead he expatiates a lot about comparison theoretically without offering us any clear and engaged textual or other examples. This, as I shall explain shortly, is the major issue that I have with CSR and its approach to comparison: while it may sound scientific and precise, it offers precious little insight about specific contexts that are one of the hallmarks of specialized study. If CSR moves from specific groups to the supra-level of the human species, it unfortunately also moves from the specialized and technical study needed to study specific groups to a scientific jargon that minimizes them.

Within this context, CSR presents itself, in the words of Claire White, as "a theory that human cognition is necessary (but not sufficient) to explain the persistence and prevalence of human ideas and behaviors deemed 'religious'" (White 2017: 95).[3] CSR would seem to emerge from a perceived general dissatisfaction with our basic assumptions and explanations of how cultural concepts (including, of course, religion) are both acquired and transmitted in culture. For scholars in CSR, again in the words of White, "what constitutes religious systems is an assortment of recurring psychological predispositions and behaviors, expressed in a myriad of ways with differential environmental inputs" (*ibid.*: 99). Through the application of contemporary theories of how the mind works and the use of scientific methods to test these ideas, scholars engaged in CSR seek to demonstrate what they consider to be several stable features of religion. One such feature, at least for them, is how particular kinds of ideas and behaviors persist in relatively stable forms throughout history and across different cultural environments (e.g., Sperber 1996). Another feature is why some ideas are especially prevalent over others within and across traditions (e.g., Boyer 2003: 119).

Methodologically, this has seen those interested in CSR shift their focus from text to laboratory and from specific and localized contexts to the entire human species. Some even seek to employ, among other things, brain-imaging technologies to understand the neural correlates activated in religious cognition and experiences (e.g., Andersen *et al.* 2014). While they may use what they consider to be cutting edge scientific theory, many of those involved with CSR are incapable of reading texts in their original languages, in addition to the fact that they run roughshod over the historical record. These two lacunae translate into a fundamental inability on their part to appeal to those who actually work in these areas.[4] These latter three criteria, I have emphasized time and again in the previous pages, are crucial to the comparative enterprise.

In its attempt to account for the persistence and prevalence of religious ideas, CSR, as we have seen, raises analysis to the level of the species, trying to account for panhuman cognitive predispositions. Such dispositions, it is maintained, correspond to intuitions that all humans share with minimal instruction, even though their expression may be modified by cultural input (see, e.g., McCauley 2011). This talk of the panhuman quest for meaning, and an underlying set of patterns that govern this quest, should, at least when stripped of its scientific verbiage, remind us of a discourse with which we should now be quite familiar.

In this respect CSR's search for patterns is, at least in theory, not qualitatively different from that found in phenomenology or neo-phenomenology. While these are certainly not the same patterns that Eliade looked for, they are, like his, nevertheless largely dehistoricized and are assumed to exist naturally in the world, ready for the scholar to isolate and interpret them. In his critique of CSR, for example, Russell McCutcheon writes

> What therefore troubles me about the attempt to find religious experiences in the mind/brain or religion in the genes is the manner in which, despite the sophistication that informs its use, a culturally and historically local nomenclature (i.e., this is religion, that is not religion) is being dehistoricized and thus normalized by being medicalized and thus naturalized. (McCutcheon 2010: 1185)

In the quest to reduce religion to cognition and behavior, however, McCutcheon notes that CSR paradoxically risks further reifying the concept. CSR, not unlike other theories of religion, remains premised on the assumption that belief in superhuman agents constitutes "religion" and then subsequently categorizes human actions and behaviors around these beliefs. Such assumptions, however, are of limited value in the study of social groups trying to carve out meaning for themselves in light of the complexity of actual historical and social contexts such as witnessed in my extended example from the previous chapter.

To return briefly to that example, it strikes me that CSR is unable to account for the complexity of overlapping social forms existing on the margins just as it is simultaneously unable to illumine the establishment of orthodoxy (e.g., the Babylonian Talmud) at the center. This failure makes it fundamentally unable or unwilling to address many of the issues that the comparative project ideally tries to answer. Scholars associated with CSR might respond that they have conducted research with children and adults in the lab, both within and across cultures, to understand early cognitive biases as they are relatable to religious ideas and practices (e.g., Cohen 2007; Astuti and Harris 2008; Emmons and Kelemen 2014). While this may provide us with a modicum of understanding about how and why children reason about—and respond to—phenomena that are perceived to be staples of religion, such as gods and supernatural agents, left unaccounted for is who determines what is or is not constructed as "religious" in the first place. As Matt Sheedy writes:

> If, for example, a small child living in contemporary Atlanta hears a bump in the night and attributes some sort of agency to it, the explanations that she contrives or is told by her parents may have nothing at all to do with what is conventionally termed "religion." For ideas to be deemed religious requires a particular context within which this child has been socialized, leaving me to wonder whether so-called "religious ideas" [actually] arise from ... "panhuman cognitive predispositions." (Sheedy 2017: 125)

In order to counter the claims that they lack the skills to deal with the historical record, other scholars of CSR have sought to conduct secondary analyses of historical databases, such as the Standard Cross-Cultural Sample (SCCS), the Human Relations Area Files (HRAF), or the Database for Religious History (DRH).[5] Databases such as these, it is believed, make possible both synchronic and diachronic comparative analyses. Again, though, I am skeptical. While such databases may offer a modicum of utility to consult data, the question remains, whose data? Why this data and not that? Databases, of course, also provide us with reams of context-less material, whereas I have tried to argue that central to the comparative enterprise is context. It is only by understanding such contexts that we can appreciate particular social facts and then, if able or necessary, to illumine how the particular relates to more universal questions. For some, these universal questions may derive from CSR, but they do not have to.

These criticisms do not mean the CSR cannot ever play a role in the comparative enterprise. At some point in the future, this theoretical orientation may very well provide insights, but it is necessary for those who work in this area to be aware of what they can realistically do and what they cannot. As it stands at the current moment, scholars involved in CSR have overstated their case and, despite appeals to the contrary, the majority are poorly equipped to engage in the type of thick contextual work that I have argued ought to be one of the hallmarks of the comparative enterprise. Even those that do work in specific contexts (e.g., Whitehouse 1995; Cohen 2007; Xygalatas 2014) work only with contemporary forms, and I am not sure if they are equipped to work with canonical texts—such as the Qur'an or the Talmud—from the past. I have yet to see a work produced by CSR that would provide me any insight into the social formation of Muslim and Jewish groups in the aftermath of Muhammad's death. I do not rule out, however, that this may change in the coming years, but at the present moment I remain skeptical.

Even if religion can be explained "scientifically," regardless of cultural context, I am not certain that we will find ourselves in a situation in which we any better understand the historical and textual process that we possess from social groups to make sense of their social worlds. Certainly CSR might help us understand *some* of the cognitive process and behaviors whereby humans adapt to their immediate natural environments, but I have serious reservations that CSR will help us better understand groups like the Isawiyya that I examined in the second half of the previous chapter.

Conclusions

This chapter has sought to show that there exist various types of comparisons and comparative models. Some are certainly more analytic than others, and some more grounded in historical, textual, and linguistic contexts than others. It is imperative that, no matter what model one chooses, there are certain features that must reside at the heart of the modern comparative enterprise. At the risk of repeating myself, these are:

1. Sensitivity to the historical record. One cannot use history as a plaything upon which one can transpose modern virtues and ideas. Presentism always lurks in the shadows of scholarship in religious studies—the historical record is used when necessary or convenient, and marginalized or truncated when not—but it cannot. To appreciate this historical record, however, one must have the full range of scholarly competences (linguistic, textual, manuscript, social, cultural, and so on). But, and this is important, this is but one item. Too much emphasis on this can lead to historical positivism.

2. Linguistic dexterity, which in turn promotes as wide a knowledge as possible of the relevant textual and manuscript traditions necessary for the particular context one studies. One must know the languages in which one ostensibly works. One, quite simply, cannot do comparative work with English translations. If one does not want to learn languages, then, at the risk of sounding overly exclusive, the only option is to work, as many increasingly do, in the idiom of religion/s in America.

3. Theoretical sophistication. This is what differentiates—or ought to differentiate—the scholar of religion from the historian, the philologist, and the scholar of area studies. This means being aware of the conceit of comparison while simultaneously engaging in it.

These three elements ought to form our collective enterprise. They are what allow us to talk to one another while also being able to talk to those who work on our data but do so outside the disciplinary confines of religious studies.

* * *

I hope that this slim volume has made the case as to why comparison has the potential to be such an important part of the academic study of religion. Any acknowledgment of this importance, however, has to come with an understanding of this method's past. Used in the service of a host of dubious and prejudicial causes, comparison has been anything but a reliable method. Muted third-terms, hidden agendas, and idiosyncratic comparanda have all been used and abused for intellectually and morally suspect purposes. A rehabilitated comparison will ideally avoid such pitfalls because it will be honest about what is to be compared, when, why, and for what purposes. The way to move forward, this volume has suggested, is to keep comparison small and contextual. Comparison, in the final analysis, is about having the technical skill of the specialist and the theoretical sophistication of the social theorist. One without the other is not comparison. This future, I hope, will also see comparison used as a rigorous and analytical method and not idiosyncratically in the service of improving the planet's spiritual health.

Notes

1. For a critique of CSR along these lines, see Stoddard (2017).
2. There certainly are examples that do not do this. Probably the most famous in rabbinics is the work and scholarship of Jacob Neusner, who did more than anyone to bring the technical study of post-biblical Jewish texts into conversation with the academic study of religion. For details see Hughes (2016a, 2016b).
3. I find White (2017), which offers a synthetic approach and historiographical survey to CSR, a convenient introduction into this subfield.
4. Perhaps the most egregious example in my own subfield of Jewish studies of this simultaneous inability to deal adequately with the textual evidence and appeal to those who actually work in the field is Levy (2013).
5. See the comments in Slingerland and Sullivan (in press) for an overview of this approach to "historical" research.

Further Reading

General Works

Littleton, C. Scott. 1973. *The New Comparative Mythology: An Anthropological Assessment of the Theories of Georges Dumézil* (revised edition). Berkeley, CA: University of California Press.

Patton, Laurie C., and Benjamin C. Ray (eds). 2000. *A Magic Still Dwells: Comparative Religion in the Postmodern Age*. Berkeley, CA: University of California Press.

Preus, J. Samuel. 1987. *Explaining Religion: Criticism and Theory from Bodin to Freud*. New Haven, CT: Yale University Press.

Sharpe, Eric. J. 1975. *Comparative Religion: A History*. London: Duckworth.

Smith, Jonathan Z. 1978. *Map is Not Territory: Studies in the History of Religions*. Chicago, IL: University of Chicago Press.

Smith, Jonathan Z. 1982. "In Comparison a Magic Dwells." In his *Imagining Religion: From Babylon to Jonestown*, 19–35. Chicago, IL: University of Chicago Press.

Smith, Jonathan Z. 1990. *Drudgery Divine: On the Comparison of Early Christianities and the Religions of Late Antiquity*. Chicago, IL: University of Chicago Press.

Classic Phenomenological Approaches

Campbell, Joseph. [1949]2008. *The Hero With a Thousand Faces*. Novato, CA: New World Books.

Eliade, Mircea. 1958. *Patterns in Comparative Religion*. Trans. Rosemary Sheed. New York: Sheed & Ward.

Smith, Huston. 1958[1991]. *The World's Religions*. New York: HarperCollins.

© Equinox Publishing Ltd. 2017

Comparison and Ideology

Arvidsson, Stefan. 2006. *Aryan Idols: Indo-European Mythology as Ideology and Science*. Trans. Sonia Wichmann. Chicago, IL: University of Chicago Press.
Chidester, David. 1996. *Savage Systems: Colonialism and Comparative Religion in Southern Africa*. Charlottesville, VA: University of Virginia Press.
Chidester, David. 2014. *Empire of Religion: Imperialism and Comparative Religion*. Chicago, IL: University of Chicago Press.
Dubuisson, Daniel. 2003. *The Western Construction of Religion: Myths, Knowledge, and Ideology*. Trans. William Sayers. Baltimore, MD: Johns Hopkins University Press.
Fitzgerald, Timothy. 2000. *The Ideology of Religious Studies*. New York: Oxford University Press.
Hughes, Aaron W. 2015b. "The Politics of Biblical Interpretation: A Review Essay." *Critical Research on Religion* 3.3: 282–296.
Junginger, Horst (ed.). 2008. *The Study of Religion Under the Impact of Fascism*. Leiden: Brill.
Lincoln, Bruce. 1999. *Theorizing Myth: Narrative, Ideology, and Scholarship*. Chicago, IL: University of Chicago Press.

Specific Comparisons

Beard, Mary, John A. North, and S. R. F. Price. 1998. *Religions of Rome*. Cambridge: Cambridge University Press.
Bowersock, Glen Warren. 2012. *Empires in Collision in Late Antiquity*. Waltham, MA: Brandeis University Press.
Boyarin, Daniel. 2014. *Border Lines: The Partition of Judaeo-Christianity*. Philadelphia, PA: University of Pennsylvania Press.
Cameron, Averil. 2012. *The Mediterranean World in Late Antiquity: AD 395-700* (2nd edition). Abingdon: Routledge.
Crone, Patricia. 2016. "Jewish Christianity and the Qurʾān." *Journal of Near Eastern Studies* 74: 225–253.
Goitein, Shlomo Dov. 1988. *A Mediterranean Society: The Jewish Communities of the Arab World As Portrayed in the Documents of the Cairo Genizah*. 6 vols. Berkeley, CA: University of California Press
Hughes, Aaron W. 2017. *Shared Identities: Medieval and Modern Imaginings of Judeo-Islam*. New York: Oxford University Press.
Wasserstrom, Steven M. 1995. *Between Muslim and Jew: The Problem of Symbiosis Under Early Islam*. Princeton, NJ: Princeton University Press.

Cognitive Science of Religion

Boyer, Pascal. 2001. *Religion Explained: The Evolutionary Origins of Religious Thought*. New York: Basic Books.

McCauley, Robert N. 2011. *Why Religion is Natural and Science is Not*. New York: Oxford University Press.

McCutcheon, Russell T. 2010. "Will Your Cognitive Anchor Hold in the Storms of Culture?" *Journal of the American Academy of Religion*. 78.4: 1182–1193.

Paden, William E. 2016. *New Patterns for Comparative Religion: Passages to an Evolutionary Perspective*. London: Bloomsbury.

References

Abu Nimer, Mohammed, Amal Khoury, and Emily Welty. 2007. *Unity in Diversity: Interfaith Dialogue in the Middle East*. Washington, DC: United States Institute of Peace.

Ackerman, Susan. 2010. "Only Men are Created Equal." *Journal of Hebrew Scriptures* 10: article 9. Retrieved from www.jhsonline.org/Articles/article_137.pdf.

Andersen, M., U. Schjødt, K. L. Nielbo, and J. Sørensen. 2014. "Mystical Experience in the Lab." *Method and Theory in the Study of Religion* 26.3: 217–245.

Arjomand, Said Amir. 1994. "Abd Allah Ibn al-Muqaffa' and the Abbasid Revolution." *Religion and Society in Islamic Iran during the Pre-Modern Era* 27.1: 9–36.

Arnal, William E., and Russell T. McCutcheon. 2013. *The Sacred is the Profane: The Political Nature of "Religion."* New York: Oxford University Press.

Arvidsson, Stefan. 2006. *Aryan Idols: Indo-European Mythology as Ideology and Science*. Trans. Sonia Wichmann. Chicago, IL: University of Chicago Press.

Arvidsson, Stefan. 2013. "Review of *The Cambridge Companion to Religious Studies*, Robert A. Orsi (ed.)." *Religion* 43.4: 586–590.

Asatryan, Mushegh. 2016. *Cosmology and Community in Early Shiʿi Islam: The Ghulat and their Literature*. London: I. B. Tauris.

Astuti, Ritta and Paul L. Harris. 2008. "Understanding Mortality and the Life of the Ancestors in Rural Madagascar." *Cognitive Science* 32.4: 713–740.

al-Azmeh, Aziz. 2014. *The Emergence of Islam in Late Antiquity: Allāh and His People*. Cambridge: Cambridge University Press.

Beard, Mary, John A. North, and S. R. F. Price. 1998. *Religions of Rome*. Cambridge: Cambridge University Press.

Berman, Joshua A. 2008. *Created Equal: How the Bible Broke with Ancient Political Thought*. Oxford: Oxford University Press.

Bodian, Miriam. 1999. *Hebrews of the Portuguese Nation: Conversos and Community in Early Modern Amsterdam*. Bloomington, IN: Indiana University Press.

Bowersock, Glen Warren. 2012. *Empires in Collision in Late Antiquity*. Waltham, MA: Brandeis University Press.

Boyarin, Daniel. 2014. *Border Lines: The Partition of Judaeo-Christianity*. Philadelphia, PA: University of Pennsylvania Press.

Boyer, Pascal. 2003. "Religious Thought and Behavior as By-products of Brain Function." *Trends in Cognitive Sciences* 7.3: 119–124.

Brakke, David. 2011. *The Gnostics: Myth, Ritual, and Diversity in Early Christianity*. Cambridge, MA: Harvard University Press.

Bryant, Edwin. 2001. *The Quest for the Origins of Vedic Culture: The Indo-Aryan Migration Debate*. Oxford: Oxford University Press.

Budde, Karl. 1899. *Religion of Israel to the Exile*. New York: G. P. Putnam.

Cameron, Averil. 2012. *The Mediterranean World in Late Antiquity: AD 395–700* (2nd edition). Abingdon: Routledge.

Campbell, Joseph. [1949]2008. *The Hero With a Thousand Faces*. Novato, CA: New World Books.

Campbell, Joseph (with Bill Moyers). 1988. *The Power of Myth*. New York: Doubleday.

Casadio, Giovanni. 2011. "Raffaele Pettazzoni a Cinquant'anni dalla morte." *Studi e Materiali di Storia delle religioni* 77.1: 27–37.

Castro, Américo. [1948]1971. *The Spaniards*. Trans. Williard F. King and Selma Margaretten. Berkeley, CA: University of California Press.

Chidester, David. 1996. *Savage Systems: Colonialism and Comparative Religion in Southern Africa*. Charlottesville, VA: University of Virginia Press.

Chidester, David. 2014. *Empire of Religion: Imperialism and Comparative Religion*. Chicago, IL: University of Chicago Press.

Ciurtin, Eugen. 2008. "Raffaele Pettazzoni et Mircea Eliade. Historiens des religions généralistes devant les fascismes (1933–1945)." In Horst Junginger (ed.), *The Study of Religion Under the Impact of Fascism*, 333–363. Leiden: Brill.

Clooney, Francis. X. 2005. *Divine Mother, Blessed Mother: Hindu Goddesses and the Virgin Mary*. New York: Oxford University Press.

Cohen, Emma. 2007. *The Mind Possessed: The Cognition of Spirit Possession in an Afro-Brazilian Religious Tradition*. New York: Oxford University Press.

Cohen, Gerson. 1974. "Rabbinic Judaism (2nd–18th Centuries)." In *Encyclopedia Britannica* (15th edition), vol. 22: 416–422.

Crone, Patricia. 2016. "Jewish Christianity and the Qurʾān." *Journal of Near Eastern Studies* 74: 225–253.

Dempsey, Corinne G. 2012. *Bringing the Sacred Down to Earth: Adventures in Comparative Religion*. New York: Oxford University Press.

Donne, John. c.1611. "A Valediction: Forbidding Mourning." Retrieved from www.poetryfoundation.org/poems-and-poets/poems/detail/44131.
Dubuisson, Daniel. [1993]2006. *Twentieth Century Mythologies: Dumézil, Lévi-Strauss, Eliade* (2nd edition). Trans. Martha Cunningham. London: Equinox.
Dubuisson, Daniel. 2003. *The Western Construction of Religion: Myths, Knowledge, and Ideology*. Trans. William Sayers. Baltimore, MD: Johns Hopkins University Press.
Durkheim, Émile. [1915]1965. *The Elementary Forms of the Religious Life*. Trans. Joseph Ward Swain. New York: The Free Press.
El-Badawi, Emran. 2013. *The Qur'an and the Aramaic Gospel Traditions*. Abingdon: Routledge.
Eliade, Mircea. 1958. *Patterns in Comparative Religion*. Trans. Rosemary Sheed. New York: Sheed & Ward.
Emmons, Natalie A. and Deborah Kelemen. 2014. "The Development of Children's Prelife Reasoning: Evidence from Two Cultures." *Child Development* 85.4: 1617–1633.
Feldman, Louis H. 1993. *Jew and Gentile in the Ancient World: Attitudes and Interactions from Alexander to Justinian*. Princeton, NJ: Princeton University Press.
Fitzgerald, Timothy. 2000. *The Ideology of Religious Studies*. New York: Oxford University Press.
Funk, Nathan C., and Meena Sharify Funk. 2009. "Peacemaking Among the Children of Abraham: Overcoming Obstacles to Co-existence." In Moshe Ma'oz (ed.), *The Meeting of Civilizations: Muslim, Christian, and Jewish*, 203–219. Eastbourne: Sussex Academic Press.
Gandini, Mario. 1960. "Nota bibliografica degli scritti de Rafaelle Pettazzoni." *Studi e Materiali di Storia dell Religioni* 31: 3–21.
Geertz, Clifford. 1973. "Thick Description: Toward an Interpretative Theory of Culture." In his *The Interpretation of Cultures*, 3–30. New York: Basic Books.
Gill, Brendan. 1989. "The Faces of Joseph Campbell." *The New York Review of Books* 36.14 (September 28).
Goitein, Shlomo Dov. 1955. *Jews and Arabs: Their Contact Through the Ages* (3rd edition). New York: Schocken.
Goitein, Shlomo Dov. 1974. "Religion in Everyday Life as Reflected in the Documents of the Cairo Genizah." In S. D. Goitein (ed.), *Religion in a Religious Age*, 3–17. Cambridge, MA: Association for Jewish Studies.
Goitein, Shlomo Dov. 1967-93. *A Mediterranean Society: The Jewish Communities of the Arab World as Portrayed in the Documents of the Cairo Genizah*. 6 vols. Berkeley, CA: University of California Press.

Grossman, Avraham. 1984. *The Babylonian Exilarchate in the Gaonic Period* (in Hebrew). Jerusalem: Zalman Shazar Center.

Henderson, John B. 1991. *Scripture, Canon and Commentary: A Comparison of Confucian and Western Exegesis*. Princeton, NJ: Princeton University Press.

Henderson, John B. 1998. *The Construction of Orthodoxy and Heresy: Neo-Confucian, Islamic, Jewish, and Early Christian Patterns*. Albany, NY: State University of New York Press.

Herodotus. 1890. *The Histories*. Trans. G. C. Macaulay. London: Macmillan & Co. Retrieved from http://wps.pearsoncustom.com/wps/media/objects/2426/2484749/chap_assets/bookshelf/herodotus.pdf.

Heschel, Susannah. 2008. *The Aryan Jesus: Christian Theologians and the Bible in Nazi Germany*. Princeton, NJ: Princeton University Press.

Howard-Johnston, James. 2011. *Witnesses to a World Crisis: Historians and Histories of the Middle East in the Seventh Century*. Oxford: Oxford University Press.

Hughes, Aaron W. 2004. *The Texture of the Divine: Imagination in Medieval Islamic and Jewish Thought*. Bloomington, IN: Indiana University Press.

Hughes, Aaron W. 2007. *The Art of Dialogue in Jewish Philosophy*. Bloomington, IN: Indiana University Press.

Hughes, Aaron W. 2012. *Abrahamic Religions: On the Uses and Abuses of History*. Oxford: Oxford University Press.

Hughes, Aaron W. 2013. *The Study of Judaism: Identity, Authenticity, Scholarship*. Albany, NY: State University of New York Press.

Hughes, Aaron W. 2015a. *Islam and the Tyranny of Authenticity: An Inquiry into Disciplinary Apologetics and Self-Deception*. Sheffield: Equinox.

Hughes, Aaron W. 2015b. "The Politics of Biblical Interpretation: A Review Essay." *Critical Research on Religion* 3.3: 282–296.

Hughes, Aaron W. 2016a. *Jacob Neusner on Religion: The Example of Judaism*. Abingdon: Routledge.

Hughes, Aaron W. 2016b. *Jacob Neusner: An American Jewish Iconoclast*. New York: New York University Press.

Hughes, Aaron W. 2017. *Shared Identities: Medieval and Modern Imaginings of Judeo-Islam*. New York: Oxford University Press.

Jevons, Frank Byron. 1908. *An Introduction to the Study of Comparative Religion*. New York: The Macmillan Company.

Junginger, Horst (ed.). 2008. *The Study of Religion Under the Impact of Fascism*. Leiden: Brill.

Junod (Arbell), Dominique-D. 2012. *Convivencia and Its French and English Equivalents: The Word and the Concept*. Trans. Martin Hemmings. Paris: Editions Florent HUET.

King, Richard. 1999. "Orientalism and the Modern Myth of 'Hinduism.'" *Numen* 46.2: 146–185.

Kripal, Jeffrey J. 2014. *Comparing Religions*. Malden, MA: Wiley-Blackwell.

Lakoff, George, and Mark Johnson. 1980. *Metaphors We Live By*. Chicago, IL: University of Chicago Press.

Laskier, Michael M., and Yaakov Lev (eds). 2011a. *The Convergence of Judaism and Islam: Religious, Scientific, and Cultural Dimensions*. Gainesville, FL: University Press of Florida.

Laskier, Michael M., and Yaakov Lev (eds). 2011b. *The Divergence of Judaism and Islam: Interdependence, Modernity, and Political Turmoil*. Gainesville, FL: University Press of Florida.

Lecker, Michael. 1995. *Muslims, Jews, and Pagan: Studies in Early Islamic Medina*. Leiden: Brill.

Lecker, Michael. 2005. "Were the Jewish Tribes in Arabia Clients of Arab Tribes?" In Monique Bernards and John Nawas (eds), *Patronate and Patronage in Early and Classical Islam*, 50–69. Leiden: Brill.

Levy, Gabriel. 2013. *Judaic Technologies of the Word: A Cognitive Analysis of Jewish Cultural Formation*. Abingdon: Routledge.

Lewis, Bernard. 1950. "An Apocalyptic Vision of Islamic History." *BSOAS* 13: 308–338

Lewis, Bernard. 1984. *The Jews of Islam*. Princeton, NJ: Princeton University Press.

Lincoln, Bruce. 1991. *Death, War, and Sacrifice: Studies in Ideology and Practice*. Chicago, IL: University of Chicago Press.

Lincoln, Bruce. 1999. *Theorizing Myth: Narrative, Ideology, and Scholarship*. Chicago, IL: University of Chicago Press.

Littleton, C. Scott. 1973. *The New Comparative Mythology: An Anthropological Assessment of the Theories of Georges Dumézil* (revised edition). Berkeley, CA: University of California Press.

Livne-Kafri, Ofer. 2001. "The Early Shiʿa and Jerusalem." *Arabica* 48: 112–120.

Livne-Kafri, Ofer. 2006. "Jerusalem in Early Islam: The Eschatological Aspect." *Arabica* 53: 382–403.

Lobel, Diana. 2011. *The Quest for God and the Good: World Philosophy as a Living Experience*. New York: Columbia University Press.

Maimonides, Moses. 1985. "Epistle to Yemen." In his *Epistles of Maimonides: Crisis and Leadership*. Trans. Abraham Halkin. Philadelphia, PA: Jewish Publication Society of America.

Masuzawa, Tomoko. 2005. *The Invention of World Religions: Or, How European Universalism Was Preserved in the Language of Pluralism*. Chicago, IL: University of Chicago Press.

Mazuz, Haggai. 2014. *The Religious and Spiritual Life of the Jews of Medina*. Leiden: Brill.

McCalla, Arthur. 1994. "When Is History Not History?" *Historical Reflections* 20.3: 435–452.

McCauley, Robert N. 2011. *Why Religion is Natural and Science is Not.* New York: Oxford University Press.

McCutcheon, Russell T. 1997. *Manufacturing Religion: The Discourse on Sui Generis Religion and the Politics of Nostalgia.* New York: Oxford University Press.

McCutcheon, Russell T. 2010. "Will Your Cognitive Anchor Hold in the Storms of Culture?" *Journal of the American Academy of Religion.* 78.4: 1182–1193.

McGuire, Meredith B. 2008. *Lived Religion: Faith and Practice in Everyday Life.* New York: Oxford University Press.

Meddeb, Abdelwahab and Benjamin Stora (eds). 2013. *A History of Jewish-Muslim Relations: From the Origins to the Present Day.* Paris/Princeton, NJ: Albin Michel/Princeton University Press.

Menocal, Maria Rosa. 2003. *The Ornament of the World: How Muslims, Jews and Christians Created a Culture of Tolerance in Medieval Spain.* New York: Back Books.

Müller, Friedrich Max, and Georgina Adelaide Müller. 1902. *The Life and Letters of the Right Honourable Friedrich Max Müller*, vol. 1. London: Longmans, Green, & Co.

Nanini, Riccardo. 2003. "Raffaele Pettazzoni e la fenomenologia della religione." *Studia Patavina* 50: 377–413.

Nanini, Riccardo. 2012. "Law and Freedom. Raffaele Pettazzoni's attitude toward Gerardus van der Leeuw's Phenomenology of Religion." *Rivista di Storia delle religioni* 19: 81-97.

Neusner, Jacob. 1991. *Rabbinic Political Theory: Religion and Politics in the Mishnah.* Chicago, IL: University of Chicago Press.

Newby, Gordon D. 1988. *A History of the Jews of Arabia: From Ancient Times to Their Eclipse under Islam.* Columbia, SC: University of South Carolina Press.

Orsi, Robert A. 2011. "The Problem of the Holy." In Robert A. Orsi (ed.), *The Cambridge Companion to Religious Studies*, 84–106. Cambridge: Cambridge University Press.

Otto, Rudolph. [1917]1923. *The Idea of the Holy: An Inquiry into the Non-rational Factor in the Idea of the Divine and its Relation to the Rational.* Trans. John W. Harvey. Oxford: Oxford University Press.

Paden, William E. 2016. *New Patterns for Comparative Religion: Passages to an Evolutionary Perspective.* London: Bloomsbury.

Patton, Laurie C., and Benjamin C. Ray. 2000. "Introduction." In Laurie C. Patton and Benjamin C. Ray (eds), *A Magic Still Dwells: Comparative Religion in the Postmodern Age*, 1–22. Berkeley, CA: University of California Press.

Pennington, Brian K. 2005. *Was Hinduism Invented? Britons, Indians, and the Colonial Construction of Religion.* New York: Oxford University Press.

Pettazzoni, Raffaele. 1912. *La religione primitiva in Sardegna.* Rome: Piacenza Società editrice pontremolese.

Pettazzoni, Raffaele. 1938. "Gli studi storico-religiosi in Italia." *Civiltà fascista* 5: 194–197.
Pettazzoni, Raffaele. 1955. *The All-knowing God: Researches Into Early Religion and Culture.* Trans. H. J. Rose. London: Methuen & Co.
Pines, Shlomo. 1966. "The Jewish Christians of the Early Centuries of Christianity According to a New Source." *Proceedings of the Israel Academy of Sciences and Humanities* 2.13: 237–310.
Plate, S. Brent (ed.). 2015. *Key Terms in Material Religion.* London: Bloomsbury.
Prandi, Carlo. 2012. "Raffaele Pettazzoni tra storicismo e fenomenologia: derive ideologiche." In Gian Pietro Basello, Paolo Ognibene, and Antonio Panaino (eds), *Il mistero che rivelato ci divide e sofferto ci unisce. Studi in onore di Mario Gandini,* 387–397. Milan: Mimesis.
Preus, J. Samuel. 1987. *Explaining Religion: Criticism and Theory from Bodin to Freud.* New Haven, CT: Yale University Press.
Promey, Sally M. (ed.). 2014. *Sensational Religion.* New Haven, CT: Yale University Press.
Prothero, Stephen. 2010. *God Is Not One: The Eight Rival Religions That Run the World—and Why Their Differences Matter.* New York: Harper One.
Roberts, Michelle Voss. 2014. *Tastes of the Divine: Hindu and Christian Theologies of Emotion.* New York: Fordham University Press.
Said, Edward W. 1975. *Orientalism.* New York: Pantheon.
Segal, Robert A. 1992. "Joseph Campbell on Jews and Judaism." *Religion* 22.2: 151–170.
Sells, Michael A. 1994. *Mystical Languages of Unsaying.* Chicago, IL: University of Chicago Press.
Severino, Valerio S. 2002. "Giovanni Gentile e Raffaele Pettazzoni (1922–1924): Un carteggio sull storia delle religioni e l'università in Italia." *Storiografia* 6: 107–126.
Sharon, Moshe. 1983. *Black Banners from the East: The Establishment of the Abbasid State: Incubation of a Revolt.* Jerusalem/Leiden: Magnes Press/Brill.
Sharpe, Eric. J. 1975. *Comparative Religion: A History.* London: Duckworth.
Sheedy, Matt. 2017. "Of Elephants and Riders: Cognition, Reason, and Will in the Study of Religion." In Aaron W. Hughes (ed.), *Theory in a Time of Excess: Beyond Reflection and Explanation in Religious Studies Scholarship,* 121–128. Sheffield: Equinox.
Shoemaker, Stephen J. 2011. *The Death of a Prophet: The End of Muhammad's Life and the Beginnings of Islam.* Philadelphia, PA: University of Pennsylvania Press.
Slingerland, Edward and Brenton Sullivan. In press. "Durkheim with Data: The Database of Religious History (DRH)." *Journal of the American Academy of Religion.*

Smith, Jonathan Z. 1978a. "Adde Parvum Parvo Magnus Acervus Erit." In his *Map is Not Territory: Studies in the History of Religions*, 240-264. Chicago, IL: University of Chicago Press.
Smith, Jonathan Z. 1978b. "The Wobbling Pivot." In his *Map is Not Territory: Studies in the History of Religions*, 88-103. Chicago, IL: University of Chicago Press.
Smith, Jonathan Z. 1982. "In Comparison a Magic Dwells." In his *Imagining Religion: From Babylon to Jonestown*, 19-35. Chicago, IL: University of Chicago Press.
Smith, Jonathan Z. 1987. *To Take Place: Toward Theory in Ritual*. Chicago, IL: University of Chicago Press.
Smith, Jonathan Z. 1990. *Drudgery Divine: On the Comparison of Early Christianities and the Religions of Late Antiquity*. Chicago, IL: University of Chicago Press.
Sperber, Dan. 1996. *Explaining Culture*. Oxford: Blackwell Publishers.
Stausberg, Michael. 2008a. "Raffaele Pettazzoni and the History of Religions in Fascist Italy (1928-1938)." In Horst Junginger (ed.), *The Study of Religion Under the Impact of Fascism*, 365-395. Leiden: Brill.
Stausberg, Michael. 2008b. "The Study of Religion(s) in Western Europe (II): Institutional Developments after World War II." *Religion* 38.4: 305-318.
Steinschneider, Moritz. 1874. "Apocalypsen mit polemischer Tendenz." *ZDMG* 28: 627-659.
Stillman, Norman. 2010. *Encyclopedia of Jews in the Islamic World*. 5 vols. Leiden: Brill.
Stoddard, Brad. 2017. "'Show Me the Money': Big-Money Donors and the Cognitive Science of Religion." In Aaron W. Hughes (ed.), *Theory in a Time of Excess: Beyond Reflection and Explanation in Religious Studies Scholarship*, 115-120. Sheffield: Equinox.
Strenski, Ivan. 1987. *Four Theories of Myth in Twentieth Century History: Cassirer, Eliade, Lévi-Strauss, and Malinowski*. Iowa City, IA: University of Iowa Press.
Stroumsa, Guy G. 1985. "Gnostics and Manichaeans in Byzantine Palestine." In Elizabeth A. Livingston (ed.), *Studia Patristica* 18, 273-278. Kalamazoo, MI: Cistercian Press.
Stroumsa, Guy G. 2010. *A New Science: The Discovery of Religion in the Age of Reason*. Cambridge, MA: Harvard University Press.
Stroumsa, Guy G. 2015a. *The Making of Abrahamic Religions in Late Antiquity*. Oxford: Oxford University Press.
Stroumsa, Guy G. 2015b. "Jewish Christianity and Islamic Origins." In Behnam Sadeghi, Asad Q. Ahmed, Adam Silverstein, and Robert Hoyland (eds). *Islamic Cultures, Islamic Contexts: Essays in Honor of Patricia Crone*, 72-96. Leiden: Brill.

Stroumsa, Sarah. 2011. *Maimonides in His World: Portrait of a Mediterranean Thinker.* Princeton, NJ: Princeton University Press.
Sugirtharajah, Sharada. 2003. *Imagining Hinduism: A Postcolonial Perspective.* New York: Routledge.
Turi, Gabriele. 2002. *Il mecenate, il filosofo e il gesuita: L'Enciclopedia italiana specchio della nazione.* Bologna: Il mulino.
Tweed, Thomas A. (ed.). 1997. *Retelling US Religious History.* Berkeley, CA: University of California Press.
Tylor, Edward Burnett. 1871. *Primitive Culture: Researches into the Development of Mythology, Philosophy, Religion, Art, and Custom.* London: John Murray.
Wasserstrom, Steven M. 1988. "An Islamicate History of Religions?" *History of Religions* 27.4: 405–411.
Wasserstrom, Steven M. 1995. *Between Muslim and Jew: The Problem of Symbiosis Under Early Islam.* Princeton, NJ: Princeton University Press.
White, Claire. 2017. "What the Cognitive Science of Religion Is (and Is Not)." In Aaron W. Hughes (ed.), *Theory in a Time of Excess: Beyond Reflection and Explanation in Religious Studies Scholarship*, 95–114. Sheffield: Equinox.
Whitehouse, Harvey. 1995. *Inside the Cult: Religious Innovation and Transmission in Papua New Guinea.* New York: Oxford University Press.
Wolfson, Elliot R. 2014. *Giving Beyond the Gift: Apophasis and Overcoming Theomania.* New York: Fordham University Press.
Xygalatas, Dimitris. 2014. *The Burning Saints: Cognition and Culture in the Fire-walking Rituals of the Anastenaria.* Abingdon: Routledge.
Zellentin, Holger. 2013. *The Qurʾān's Legal Culture: The Didascalia Apostolorum as a Point of Departure.* Tübingen: Mohr Siebeck.

Index

Abrahamic religions 11, 43–44
American Academy of Religion (AAR) 54, 59, 105
American Lectures on the History of Religions (ALHR) 15, 16
anti-Semitism 5, 15
apologetics ix, 10–11, 22, 83
Arabian Peninsula (Hijaz) 47–49, 64
area studies 54, 74, 79, 85, 105–107, 112
Arvidsson, Stefan 27, 76n5

Berman, Joshua A. 70–72
Bible 30, 70–72
Boyarin, Daniel 25–26, 31–32, 82–85, 87
Budde, Karl 15–16, 17, 18, 20, 23, 82

Campbell, Joseph 1–6, 40, 58, 78, 104, 106
Campus Crusade for Christ ("Cru") viii
Chidester, David 27, 33
Christianity
  see Protestant Christianity
cognitive science of religion (CSR) xi, 3, 18, 72–73, 101, 107–11
colonialism 15, 27, 33
comparative linguistics 34–36, 52, 59–60
comparative theology 104–105
comparison
  artificiality of ix, 5, 8–9, 11–12
  conceit of the dominant 28, 33
  excesses of viii, 100, 101
  good comparisons 53–54, 57–59, 78, 90–98, 100–101, 106–107, 111–113
  and heresiology 30–34
  and phenomenology vii, 9, 67–70, 82, 98, 101, 103, 104, 105 see also neo-phenomenology
  contexts 77–99

Dempsey, Corinne G. 68–70, 74
Donne, John 9, 10
Dubuisson, Daniel 5, 42
Dumézil, Georges 39
Dumont, Louis 58
Durkheim, Émile 25, 40–42

ecumenicism 42–44, 45
Eliade, Mircea 3–6, 20–23, 36, 40, 42, 58, 70, 74, 78, 94
evolution of religion 16–17, 40–42

fascism 27, 38–39, 86
Foucault, Michel 33

Geertz, Clifford 58, 80–81, 97
Gentile, Giovanni 38
Goitein, Shlomo Dov 47–49
  see also symbiosis

Heidegger, Martin 3, 9
heresiography 26, 32
heresiology 30–34, 42, 84, 95

© Equinox Publishing Ltd. 2017

Herodotus 25, 29–30, 42
history x, 12–13, 23, 19–20, 44
holy 67–68
Husserl, Edmund 9

Indo-European 35, 39, 87
International Association for the History of Religions (IAHR) 37
Isawiyya 92–98, 111
Islam (and Islams) viii, x, xi, 5, 10, 13, 26, 28, 32, 33, 45, 47–49, 61–65, 79, 82, 84, 85, 90–98, 106

Jevons, Frank Byron 14–18, 19, 20–23, 28, 33, 43, 101
Jews 5–6, 26, 32, 47–49, 55–56, 61–65, 83, 90–98
Judaism, x, 4, 5, 10, 13, 15, 16, 17, 23, 34, 47–49, 55, 56, 61–65, 79, 82, 83, 84, 90–98, 99, 106
Jung, Carl Gustav 2–3
Junginger, Horst 27

Kitagawa, Joseph 3
Kripal, Jeffrey J. 102

language work (importance of) 74, 106–107, 111–112
late antiquity x, 25, 26, 42, 46, 58, 65–66, 82, 83, 90–98
Lincoln, Bruce 27, 39, 85–88

Maimonides 95–96
Martyr, Justin 25
McCutcheon, Russell 27, 109
Messi, Lionel 8–10
morphology 22, 42, 59, 74, 79, 101
  see also phenomenology
Muhammad xi, 61, 64, 79, 90, 92. 94, 96, 111
Müller, F. Max vii–viii, x, 34–36, 40, 43

narratives 55–61
nationalism 5, 27, 36–39, 86

neo-phenomenology xi, 70, 101, 102–105, 109
  see also phenomenology
normativity 25–26, 28, 31, 33, 48, 90
numinous 3, 19, 20, 22

Orsi, Robert A. 67–68
Otto, Rudolph 19–21, 22, 23, 27, 68

Paden William E. 55, 72–73, 74, 107–108
Pele 8–10
Pettazzoni, Raffaele 37–39, 40
phenomenology vii, xi, 9, 67–70, 82, 98, 99, 101, 103, 104, 105, 109
polemics ix, 10–11, 83
Preus, J. Samuel 25
protection 14–18, 44
Protestant Christianity 14, 15, 18, 20, 28, 33, 34, 42, 44, 67
Prothero, Stephen 56–57, 58, 59, 74

Reformation 26
reification 10, 12, 23, 27, 44, 52, 54, 56–57

sacred viii, xi, 3, 18–23, 32, 42, 44, 45, 46, 67, 68–70, 73, 74, 78, 86, 88, 98, 101, 102, 105, 107
  see also morphology, phenomenology
Said, Edward W. 33
Sanskrit 35
de la Saussaye, Pierre Daniël Chantepie vii
scientific objectivity (guise of) ix, 14–18, 21, 51, 101
Sells, Michael A. 88–89
September 11, 2001 42
al-Shahrastani 25, 26, 32–33, 93
Sharpe, Eric J. 32
Sheedy, Matt 110
Smith, Jonathan Z. 6, 15, 24n2, 24n6, 28–29, 46, 51–52, 57–59, 66, 74, 78

Star Wars 2
Stroumsa, Guy G. 26
symbiosis 47–49, 53, 62–65, 66, 90, 92, 96
   see also Goitein, Shlomo Dov

texts and contexts (importance of) 60, 74, 106–107, 111–112
third term 46, 56
Tylor, Edward Burnett (E. B.) 40, 43

uniqueness 11, 70–72

Van Gogh, Vincent 8–9
Voss Roberts, Michele 103–105

Waida, Manabu, 2
Warhol, Andy 8–9
Wasserstrom, Steven M. 26, 32–33, 93, 94–95
White, Claire 108
words 55–61

www.ingramcontent.com/pod-product-compliance
Lightning Source LLC
Chambersburg PA
CBHW071850230426
43671CB00012B/2131